No Cunningly Devised Fables

The Bible As History

NO CUNNINGLY DEVISED FABLES

Copyright © 2011 by Jan Smits, DDS

All rights reserved. Neither this publication nor any part of this publication may be reproduced or transmitted in any form or by any means, electronic or mechanical, including photocopying, recording or any information storage and retrieval system, without permission in writing from the author.

Unless otherwise indicated, all Scripture quotations are taken from the Holy Bible, King James Version, which is in the public domain. Scripture quotations marked NKJV are taken from the New King James Version / Thomas Nelson Publishers, Nashville: Thomas Nelson Publishers, Copyright 1982. Used by permission. All rights reserved.

ISBN: 978-1-77069-084-4

Word Alive Press
131 Cordite Road, Winnipeg, MB R3W 1S1
www.wordalivepress.ca

Library and Archives Canada Cataloguing in Publication

Smits, Jan, 1936–
    No cunningly devised fables : the Bible as history / Jan Smits.

Includes bibliographical references.
ISBN 978-1-77069-084-4

    1. Bible—History of Biblical events. 2. Myth in the Bible. I. Title.

BS635.3.S65 2010   220.9'5   C2010-905521-7

O fools, and slow of heart to believe all
that the prophets have spoken.

Luke 24:25

For the kingdom is the Lord's:
and he is the governor among the nations.

Psalms 22:28

Contents

Thanks	vii
Introduction	1
1. History From Beginning to End	7
2. Abraham	40
3. Israel in Egypt	47
4. How Many People in the Exodus?	56
5. From Exodus to Temple	65
6. Egypt's Second Intermediate Period	75
7. Solomon's Temple and the Divided Kingdom	87
8. Daniel's Seventy Weeks	93
9. On Revelation	113
10. The Sabbath	123
11. The Arab–Iraeli Conflict	137
Epilogue	150

Thanks

Thanks to God for his care and providence. He gave me parents who sent us to Sunday school. He gave me a grandmother who prayed, whose favourite song was "Awake, you that sleep, and arise from the dead."[1] Truly, the promise is to you and to your children (Acts 2:39). We see it fulfilled in ours. Our children made various suggestions, and one of our granddaughters even helped with the title.

Thanks to my wife Magda, who puts up with my preoccupations.

Thanks for the Pinnegar family, who prayed me into the kingdom.

Thanks for Mr. Harold Colvin, a Presbyterian minister, who taught me the Word, thus baptizing me in the name of the Father, the Son, and the Holy Ghost (Matthew 28:19).

Thanks also for all those on whose shoulders I have stood, from whose works I have profited. Not that I always agreed, but Proverbs 27:17 says: *"Iron sharpens iron, so a man sharpens the countenance of his friend"* (NKJV).

---

[1] Parson, Petro. *Psalmen en Gezangen Ned. Herv. Kerk* (Haarlem, Nederland: Johan Enschede, 1938), p. 165.

Dr. Jan Smits

Thanks to John McKay in Australia, a geologist who showed that geology does not teach evolution and woke me up to history.

Thanks to God, who made me to want and able to do this work (Philippians 2:13).

Introduction

This book began as a series of articles on the internet. They defend the theme that as Christians *"we have not followed cunningly devised fables"* (2 Peter 1:16). Humanly speaking, we may have a God, but some things in the Bible seem so fantastic that we just have to assume that the Bible uses the imagery of ancient times. These stories try to teach something, but in reality they are made up. Having personally not seen the miracles of God, and looking at the achievements of modern science, we can only assume that in the Bible we deal with myths.

This was humanly speaking. Pharaoh also said, *"Who is the Lord, that I should obey His voice to let Israel go? I do not know the Lord"* (Exodus 5:2, NKJV).

Speaking as a believer, parables indeed are made up, but other stories are not. These "myths" I will clear up. Secular recorded history can hardly go back farther than the Flood of Genesis, and it does not. Christians in general do not think of the Flood as myth. God gave us a rainbow in the sky as a sign of his faithfulness, that we might know he would not destroy the world again with a flood (Genesis 9:8–17). God gave us an ark—Jesus Christ—and the door to that ark is still open.

People, left to their own devices, will always adopt lower and lower standards (Romans 1:17–32). Thor Heyerdahl's book, *Aku–Aku: The Secret of Easter Island*,[2] unintentionally illustrates this truth. In a small world, we see history speeded up. As such, Easter Island prophesies world history. History tells us that men only fail. Our Bible tells us what God has done about it. Only Jesus saves (John 3:16).

Mankind has failed God several times in the past—in the Fall (Genesis 3), before the Flood (Genesis 6), in Babylon with its tower (Genesis 11:1–9), and with the Hebrew judges and kings. Israel returned from Babylon, but it failed again. Mankind will fail today. Pope Benedict XVI[3] recognizes a falling away of the European Union. Also the United Nations—Babylon all over again—will fail, but God gave us his only Son, that whoever trusts in him should not perish. Simply, God will condemn men because they have not believed him (John 3:18). Jesus is called the Word of God, the beginning of creation (John 1:1). He is the Gate to God, the way to heaven, the ladder upon which the angels of God ascend and descend (John 1:51).

For proper benefit, I recommend that you follow up on the longer quoted texts. Dr. Floyd Nolen Jones states, and I agree, that only Christianity can academically defend its statements.[4] At one time a pastor accused me of "keeping

---

2 Heyerdahl, Thor. *Aku–Aku: The Secret of Easter Island* (Woking and London: Unwin Brothers, Ltd., 1958).
3 "Pope blasts Europe for excluding God." *U.S. & World.* 31 October 2010 (http://foxnews.com/story/0,2933,160176.html).
4 Jones, Floyd Nolen. *The Chronology of the Old Testament* (Green Forest, AR: Masterbooks, 2005), p. iv, proposition 1, p. 7, and p. v (last

a paper pope," meaning that I honoured the word of God too much. I held up my King James Bible and quoted *"In the beginning was the Word, and the Word was with God, and the Word was God"* (John 1:1). Though the King James does not contain God's Word quite perfectly, it always shows the way of salvation (2 Timothy 3:15).

Since its first writing, indeed, since Jerome first translated the Scriptures into Latin, or even earlier, biblical scholarship has made some advances. Some myths have been around almost forever; others have been created fairly recently. I will only deal with some.

These essays may make it easier to believe the Bible. I hope to open the door a little wider into the kingdom of our Lord and Saviour (2 Peter 1:11, Psalms 84:10). God's kingdom is not a democracy. To enter in, we need to repent (Matthew 4:17). This requires faith, without which no man can please him (Hebrews 11:6). God loves a humble heart, but resists the proud. The law came by Moses, but grace and truth came by Jesus Christ (John 1:17). Moses and all the prophets spoke of him (John 5:39, 46).

Goliath thought he would slay David, but David killed him with his own sword! Likewise, mockers may think to slay "superstition" with science. They too will never admit defeat. However, those with an academic interest may find this book rewarding. Isaac Newton was a humble man. He said, "If I have seen farther than others, it is because I stood on the shoulders of giants." A Christian can say, "If I see

---

two paragraphs).

farther than others, it is because I stand on the Word of God." Fear him. He's the biggest giant of all (see Deuteronomy 10:12).

These essays do not constitute a complete defence of Scripture, but they try to answer some questions and rightly interpret the Word. They try to provide a historical overview and a message. The course of the world takes us downward, but God calls us upward. Those with ears to hear will hear that call. That's my prayer.

Jan Smits, D.D.S.
Markdale, Ontario.

No Cunningly Devised Fables

How in occupied Holland we
waited for freedom.

My soul waits for the Lord more than those who watch for the morning. (Psalms 130:6, NKJV)

Therefore if the Son makes you free, you shall be free indeed. (John 8:36, NKJV)

Chapter One

HISTORY FROM BEGINNING TO END

A Strict Chronology

Three points have a bearing on chronology and deserve attention. First, Enoch was the seventh generation from Adam (Genesis 5:3–32, Jude 14). Enoch prophesied doom, naming his son Methuselah, meaning "at his death." Methuselah died in the year of the Flood. Second, the names of the patriarchs before the Flood foretell the gospel,[5] as seen below.

Name	Meaning
1. Adam	Man
2. Seth	Appointed
3. Enos	A mourner
4. Kenon	A fallen man
5. Mahalalel	The glory of God
6. Jared	Came down

---

5   I learned this long ago at a Bill Gothard seminar, but a fuller discussion is found in Allen, Sharon R., *My Jewish Heart*, 1993. The copy of this, on one sheet of paper, was obtained through Sid Roth, http://www.sidroth.org/site/PageServer?pagename_abt_Canada.

7. Enoch	Consecrated
8. Methuselah	At his death
9. Lamech	Mighty
10. Noah	Peace

Isn't this amazing? In total, these ten men lived 2,256 years before the Flood. (See list, "Figures We Use.") God, because he knows the end from the beginning, had men give these names. Third, as we will see, the number ten is significant. While the years given diligently in Genesis 5 indicate a strict timetable, these three points confirm it. A strict timetable means that the numerical data in the Bible are genuine. It also means that these numbers should agree with each other. Note that with these names Genesis implies a second promise of a Saviour; the first promise is explicit in Genesis 3:15: *"I will put enmity between thee and the woman, and between thy seed and her seed; it shall bruise thy head, and thou shalt bruise his heel."*

MASORETIC OR SEPTUAGINT TEXT?

Biblical chronology is the study of events in the Bible in an effort to date them. In an atlas we use fixed lines—the equator and the Greenwich meridian—to locate a place. In history we use the terms B.C. and A.D., *Before Christ* and *Anno Domini* (the year of our Lord), to orientate ourselves in time. Another term is *Anno Mundi*, the year of the world, or what is almost the same, the year since creation. The events in the Old Testament, before Jesus was born, are chiefly in question.

There are two main texts of the Old Testament. The one is the Greek, or Septuagint, written LXX (the Roman form of "Seventy"—L is "fifty" and X is "ten"). The term is actually rounded off to the closest ten, since there were said to be seventy-two translators. The other main text is the Hebrew, or Masoretic, version.

Neither one is original. Sometimes the original Hebrew text is referred to as the Vorlage text, from the German, pronounced *forlaguh*. The German verb "*vorliegen*" means "to lie before." Therefore Vorlage means "what is lying in front, something to be copied."

The Septuagint, the oldest translation of the Jewish *Tenach* (essentially the Old Testament) into Greek, dates back to the third century B.C. The earliest Masoretic text is from around A.D. 900.[6] In the Masoretic text the data do not always agree with each other.

Because of God's double testimony, by which God confirmed and guarded his Word, I will mostly use the Masoretic text to verify the LXX (Septuagint). By double testimony I mean that one record is backed up by another. Two texts should not contradict each other. I look for this confirmation. According to Matthew 18:16, two or three witnesses establish a testimony. I will prove from contradictions in the King James Version that the LXX has translated certain texts correctly. Because the *original* Hebrew text was the source, the Greek text is sometimes more accurate. By

---

[6] Jones, Floyd Nolen. *The Chronology of the Old Testament* (Green Forest, AR: Masterbooks, 2005), p. 16.

the time of the Masoretes, no matter their claim to accuracy, the Hebrew text had become more corrupt than the Greek translation. The damage had been done.

Though at times I prefer the Septuagint, it also deviates. For instance, right up front, and therefore strategically, the LXX has Methuselah survive the flood for fourteen years. I consider it strategic, because Satan wants us to declare the Septuagint unreliable from the start. Actually, only eight persons survived the flood. If Methuselah survived the flood, it would make his name, "At his death," meaningless. It would mean that nine people survived the flood. This contradiction in the Septuagint is often pointed out as a glaring mistake to persuade readers to quit reading the Septuagint. Here I choose the Masoretic version. Satan is clever.

If we apply the double testimony check to the Septuagint, the LXX fails. On page 30 of *The Chronology of the Old Testament* Jones writes "However, not only are these LXX manuscripts inconsistent within themselves, omitting the second Cainan in the parallel passage 1 Chron. 1:17, the oldest Septuagint manuscripts do not include Cainan in the Genesis 11 listing. In addition, the fact that the second Cainan found in some of the LXX manuscripts has exactly the same dates assigned to him as Salah further attests to its spurious nature and militates against its being an original reading."[7] On page 32 he writes, "Many opt for Dr. Oliver R. Blosser's solution, viz. that Luke's gospel did not originally contain

---

7 Ibid, p. 30.

the name "Cainan" in verse 36"[8] (of Luke 3). The Bodmer papyrus, the oldest known copy of Luke, does not mention a second Cainan. Maybe Flosser is right in this, although Jones is a biblicist as he defines on page 31, and therefore disagrees.[9] Who tried to discredit the LXX?

In the Masoretic, God demonstrated his grace by extending a man's life to 969 years, the longest of anyone, and thereby delaying the impending Flood. Through Methuselah and Noah, God warned the world long before the Flood. He warned twice because he meant it. In Genesis 41:32, where Pharaoh has two dreams, Joseph tells him that the repetition, the double testimony, signifies that God has determined the matter and that God will bring it about quickly. We find this principle in the Bible several times. For example, John the Baptist has two texts to validate him as a prophet, Isaiah 40 and Malachi 3. Jesus approved him.

James Ussher, in writing *The Annals of the World*,[10] is the best author known to extensively write on the subject of chronology. He had the right idea that the Bible intends a strict timetable,[11] but he used the Masoretic version. He obtained 4004 B.C. as the year of creation.[12]

Though in this book I start from the beginning to the present day, I worked my way back in time. I had to start with known events before I could consider unknown ones.

8 Ibid, p. 32.
9 Ibid, p. 31.
10 Ussher, James. *The Annals of the World,* revised and updated by Larry and Marion Pierce (Green Forest, AR: Masterbooks, 2003).
11 Ibid, p. 8.
12 Ibid, p. 17.

I had heard of the concept of a double testimony, but I discovered its importance when I wrote about the Exodus. Once I realized certain details and events, I became aware of other evidence for them.

Why I Sometimes Choose the LXX

1. Age of Trees

The Masoretic text says that the Flood happened in 2348 B.C. This we determine by subtracting 1,656 (the number of years up to the death of Methuselah) from 4004, the year of creation (Genesis 5, 7:6). According to a report in National Geographic,[13] the oldest living trees started growing in 2766 B.C., long before the Flood. However, going by the LXX, these trees would have begun to grow well after the Flood. I am inclined to think that no trees survived the Flood, and I therefore adopt the LXX figures.

2. Time of Men from Flood to Babel

In the Masoretic Bible, Peleg was born 101 years after the Flood (Genesis 11:10–17). Peleg (meaning "division") got his name because in his days the earth was divided (Genesis 10:25, 11:7–9). Suddenly the builders of the tower of Babel could not understand each other and therefore quit building. Thirty years after his birth there were not enough men to undertake the project, nor were there enough to be scattered. Therefore, it would seem that this was too early for the events at the Tower of Babel. However, using the Masoretic numbers, 130 years after the Flood also

---

[13] Schulman, Edmund. *National Geographic*. March 1958. First recognized in 1954.

makes it too late, because bilingual dictionaries existed a thousand years before Moses.[14]

In contrast, according to the Greek text, the confusion of languages, the abandonment, and the dispersion would have happened over four hundred years after the Flood, not long after 2598 B.C. (see list, "Figures We Use"). By then the number of people ran into the millions. Again the LXX appears more correct.

3. Ages of Patriarchs after the Flood

Noah was six hundred years old at the time of the Flood (Genesis 7:6), and he lived after the flood another three hundred and fifty years (Genesis 9:28). From the Masoretic text we can extract the following table (Genesis 11:10–26):

	Age at Eldest Son's Birth	Years More Until Death
Shem (2 years after flood)	100	500
Arphaxad	35	403
Salah	30	403
Eber	34	430
Peleg	30	209
Reu	32	207
Serug	30	200
Nahor	29	109
Terah (at Abram's birth)	130	75

---

14 Taylor, Ian. *In the Minds of Men* (Toronto, Canada: TFE Publishing, 1984), p. 390.

Terah died at the age of 205 (Genesis 11:32). Abram then was seventy-five years old (Genesis 12:4). Abram was not the eldest.

From this Masoretic chart, we figure that Abram was born 352 years after the Flood. He lived 175 years (Genesis 25:7), and died 527 years after the Flood. Shem lived after the Flood 502 years and therefore lived until Abraham was 150 years old, ten generations down the line. Eber lived until 531 years after the Flood. That would make Eber outlive Abraham by four years. Even Noah would have lived until two years before Abram was born. It really does not make much sense.

According to our Greek numbers, Eber died 270 years after Peleg was born, when his great-grandson was eight years old. This is more likely, avoiding the problems posed in *The Genesis Flood* by Morris and Whitcomb.[15] Since the Greek's post-Flood numbers make more sense, we also use the Greek pre-Flood numbers.

FIGURES WE USE

	Age at Eldest Son's Birth	Years More Until Death
Adam	230	700
Seth	205	707
Enos	190	715
Cainan	170	740
Mahalaleel	165	730
Jared	162	800
Henoch	165	200

---

15   Morris, Henry M. and Whitcomb J.C. Jr. *The Genesis Flood* (Philadelphia, PN: P&R Publishing House, 1966), Appendix, pp. 474–489.

Methuselah	187	782 (Masoretic)
Lamech	182	595 (Masoretic)
Noah	600 (602)	450
At the flood	total 2,256 years,	2998 B.C.
Shem	100	500
Arphachsad	135	330
Salah	130	336
Eber	134 (2597 B.C.)	270
Peleg	130	209
Ragau	132	207
Serug	130	200
Nahor	179	125
Terah	70	75

I left out the second Cainan, since we ought to count ten generations from Noah to Abraham, not eleven. (We'll return to this a little later, in the section titled "Early Civilization.") Luke 3:35 includes him.

For Terah's age at Abram's birth, we consider Genesis 11:26, 11:32, 15:15, and 17:17. We should see 17:17 in light of the fact that Abram was born when Terah was seventy. Abram was already thirty years older than that. Abraham saw men's ages shorten with each passing generation, but Genesis 15:15 says, *"Thou shalt be buried in a good old age."* Therefore we should expect Abram to become at least as old as his father. He lived thirty years longer. The way records in those days were kept seems to confirm this.[16] The Samaritan text of Genesis 11:32 says that Terah died at the

---

16 Wiseman, P.J. *New Beginnings in Babylon about Genesis* (Toronto, Canada: Evangelical Publishers, Wheaton, Illinois, Van Kampen Press). Ontdekkingen over Genesis, Jan Haan, N.V. Groningen, 1960. Marshall E. Scott, London, England.

age of 145 years. Josephus writes that Terah left Ur one year later, because he hated the place where his son died.[17]

From the table, note that, with the coming of the year A.D. 2010, we have come to Anno Mundi 7264, well into the eighth millennium. To God, our ages are *"as a watch in the night"* (Psalms 90:4), but we have *no* mathematical formula that a thousand years with us equals a day with God.

4. Duration of Stay in Egypt

The Masoretic text tells us that Israel stayed in Egypt 430 years, whereas the Greek says they dwelt that long in Canaan *and* Egypt (Exodus 12:40). As I will discuss in Chapter Four, the Greek version is clearer.

5. From the Exodus to the Temple

The Masoretic text tells us that Solomon began building the temple in the 480th year after the Exodus (1 Kings 6:1); the Septuagint, however, says that it was in the 440th year (3 Kings 5:18). I discuss this further in Chapter Five. The Septuagint is correct, so again it wins.

6. Archaeology

The LXX mentions knives, used in circumcision, which were buried with Joshua (Joshua 24:30). The Masoretic text makes no mention, but such knives were found in A.D. 1870[18]

---

[17] Whiston, William. *Josephus, Antiquities of the Jews* (Grand Rapids, MI: Kregel Publications, 1960). Used by permission of the publisher. All rights reserved. Book 1, chapter VI, p. 5.

[18] Keller, Werner. *The Bible as History* (New York, NY: William Morrow and Co., 1964), pp. 155–156.

in tombs in the area where the Bible says Joshua was buried (Joshua 24:30).

7. Jeremiah 28

In looking for differences between the two versions, I found an enlightening article by Peter Ackland from Australia.[19] He compared translations of Jeremiah 28 from the Hebrew and Greek. He concluded, "There is more consensus of scholarship that the shorter text on which the Septuagint is based represents the more original and superior text of the book of Jeremiah."

8. Backtracking of History

We will trace history back to the time of the flood, agreeing with the Greek version. To not do so would mean tucking away some seven hundred years, and thus distorting history. Going by the Masoretic alone, a true historian may well conclude that the Bible must be myth. Why put faith in it?

9. Masoretic Bible Resorts to the LXX

Although some authors extol the King James Version and the Masoretic text, and disdain the Septuagint, the fact remains that the KJV in at least two instances follows the Septuagint. They are the Messianic verses *"they pierced my hands and my feet"* (Psalms 22:16) and *"a virgin shall conceive"* (Isaiah 7:14). I conclude that the Septuagint does deserve a place on the witness stand.

---

[19] Ackland, Peter. Lightpath, web. This article is no longer on the web. I refer the reader to http://en.wikipedia.org/wiki/book of Jeremiah. Read what the Jewish encyclopedia says about Emmanuel Tov.

What Happened?

Barry Setterfield, a biblical chronologist, on his website (www.scripturechronology.com) offers a beautiful and more extensive discussion of what happened at the Council of Jamnia in about A.D. 100, where the Jews tried to establish a standard text.[20] He says, "The Masoretic Hebrew can be traced directly to 100 AD." At that council, he explains, the Jews preferred the Masoretic text, because the Septuagint had become the "Bible of the Christians" (Dr. Siegfried S. Horn).

After that, they destroyed the *Vorlage*, the source of the LXX. Akiba Ben Joseph, the leader of that council, not the chairman, supported Bar Kokhba, who claimed to be the Messiah! So then, because Jesus did not bow to them or work with them, they rejected him. "The Septuagint was too messianic," meaning it pointed too much to Jesus. Jesus followed the original text, and so did the apostles mostly, if not altogether.

The Jews hated Jesus with a passion. Pilate sought to release Jesus and proclaimed him King of the Jews, Iesus Nazarenus Rex Iudaeorum (John 9:12, 22). The centurion glorified God, saying, *"This was a righteous man"* (Luke 23:47), but *"his own received him not"* (John 1:11). They cried out, *"We have no king but Caesar"* (John 19:15), a stranger, totally against the order given them in Deuteronomy 17:15. According to it, if they chose a king, he should be a born Hebrew, not a

---

20 Setterfield, Barry, *Creation and Catastrophe Chronology*, 1 November 2010, http://.dolphin.org/barrychron.html.

stranger. Truly, as Jesus said, *"They have persecuted me, they will also persecute you"* (John 15:20). Although they thought he was dead, they still persecuted Jesus, the Word. At first Paul was one of them. *"Saul, Saul, why are you persecuting Me?"* (Acts 9:4, NKJV)

The hate of the Jews whipped them on to worse and worse things. In *The Chronology of the Old Testament*, Dr. Floyd Jones[21] explains Jewish dating. The Jewish calendar rests on the *Seder Olem Rabbah*, the book of the Order of the World, compiled before A.D. 160. Using the Masoretic text, this calendar places creation at 3761 B.C. The Jews seem to have purposely messed up the chronology, and excuse themselves, helping God to *"shut up the words, and seal the book, even to the time of the end"* (Daniel 12:4). They denied that the prophecy of Daniel's seventy weeks (Daniel 9:24–27) pointed to Jesus. They backed up the messianic claims of Bar Kokhba, a Jewish freedom fighter. The Jews were misled.

This "messiah" did not do much for them. He failed, but by the denial of Jesus, *"O Jerusalem, Jerusalem... your house is left unto you desolate"* (Luke 13:34–35). Jewish scholars know the truth, but love status and choose the wide gate (Matthew 7:15). They would rather perish than acknowledge their Messiah. Indeed, "Oh Israel, repent!"[22] *"He that hath the Son hath life; and he that hath not the Son of God hath not life"* (1 John 5:12).

---

21 Jones, Floyd Nolen. *The Chronology of the Old Testament*, (Green Forest, AR: Masterbooks, 2005), pp. 295–299.
22 Ibid., p. 299.

God asked Abraham to sacrifice his son, *"whom thou lovest"* (Genesis 22:2), but he never asks us to do anything he would not do himself, and he did. The anointed Jesus was the prophet like unto Moses; he is the Lamb of God (John 1:29). All history revolves around him. Therefore we speak of B.C. and A.D.

While I hardly believe that at Jamnia the Jews purposely falsified the Scriptures, they became Satan's tools. They were offended (see Isaiah 8:14, 28:16, and Psalms 118:22) and tried to justify themselves (see Isaiah 65–66) rather than repent (Acts 2:36–41). As men choose their own ways, so God chooses their delusions (Isaiah 66:4). They did not know how to investigate inconsistencies in Scripture. They did not know about the double testimony. They would not accept anything from the Greeks, and who could prove them wrong? But God does not sleep. Though salvation is of the Jews, *"by a foolish nation I will anger you"* (Romans 10:19). Read Isaiah 29 and 2 Timothy 3. God makes the wrath of men to praise him (Psalms 76:10). God is good; all day long he stretches forth his hands to a gainsaying people (Romans 10:21); he is always ready to forgive; his mercies are new every morning (Lamentations 3:22–23).

On this spot the temple once stood.

> I will make you a waste and a reproach among the nations that are all around you, in the sight of all who pass by. So it shall be a reproach, a taunt, a lesson, and an astonishment to the nations... I, the Lord, have spoken. (Ezekiel 5:14–15, NKJV)

Unfortunately, in the West we ended up with a text we thought was perfect. However, it was not meant for the Christians. Hieronymus (Jerome) in about A.D. 400 translated the Bible into Latin from the Hebrew, catering to the Jews. He made a mistake; after all, it is a version of the Old Testament written by enemies of Christ. Later on, the Protestants also thought the Hebrew more original and authentic, and used the Masoretic text.

The Flood

From our table, "Figures We Use," we see that the Flood took place in 2998 B.C. To determine that, I added these numbers:

- The start of the temple by Solomon in: 1011 B.C.
- From there the years back to the Exodus: 440 years
- Then back to Abraham as he left Haran: 430 years
- His age then: 75 years
- and from his birth back to the Flood: 1,042 years (over 5,000 years ago)

The biblical account of the Flood covers four chapters. It includes more detail than any other Flood story does. Indeed, it has all the detail of a freshly struck coin. Of course, the fresh coin is the original, not the worn one. The Hebrews did not embellish a Babylonian myth. In his exposition of the Gilgamesh epic, Alexander Heidel[23] demonstrated the excellence of the Bible's account. As an example, he showed how only in the Bible the birds let out by Noah follow a rational sequence. A raven, a carnivorous bird, comes first. A dove, eating seed, comes second, and after weekly intervals the second time returns with an olive leaf. The third time it does not return. In the Babylonian account, we have a dove, a swallow, and a raven successively, at unmentioned intervals.

---

23 Heidel, Alexander, *The Gilgamesh Epic and Old Testament Parrallels* (Chicago, IL: University of Chicago Press, 1949). Or see: Morris, Henry M. and Whitcomb J.C. Jr. *The Genesis Flood* (Philadelphia, PN: P&R. Publishing, 1966), p. 39.

Some coins are in "mint" condition, while others lost detail.

Photos J. Smits

OTHER EVIDENCE

The Scriptures, however, are not the only record to testify to the Flood. Pre–Flood life is visible in rock fossils on the highest mountains. Valleys everywhere are much wider than the rivers that flow through them, but at one time mighty rivers flowed there and trapped much debris. Coal, oil, and gas were formed in the process. Terrestrial upheavals accompanied the flood and made the land to rise above the water. Waterfalls eroded channels in the earth, and by the length of these channels we get some idea of their age. Ian Taylor discusses Niagara Falls[24] and produces figures in accord with the Bible. The expression "5,000 years ago" keeps returning.

Space exploration has recently shown evidence of erosion by water on Mars, and some scientists have speculated that the water "from above" (Genesis 1:7 and 7:11) during the Flood came from Saturn. They reason that both Mars and the moon experienced a Flood as well. Velikovski first suggested this idea, though he never published this. Mars still

---

24 Taylor, Ian. *In the Minds of Men* (Toronto, Canada: TFE, 1984), pp. 94–95.

has underground water. On the moon, it may have all disappeared. In any case, on August 24, 2003, Mars orbited as close to Earth as it has in at least 5,000 years.[25] Since the water on Saturn became sufficiently exhausted the first time, we did not have another Flood this time. The Bible does not mention another Flood, nor are we aware of another ice age. Therefore, creation happened less than another 5,000 years back.

The water, as it ran off the land after the
Flood, formed wide valleys.

Photo J.Smits

The early Bible people grew very old, and even nowadays very old people may exhibit Neanderthal features. Those features may just be associated with very old age. Animals lived long as well and some, such as lizards, became very big. After the Flood, lifespans declined until a new balance prevailed.

25 Merzer, Martin. "Mars about to Make Closest Pass in 5000 Years." Miami Herald, August 11, 2003. Accessed: 1 November 2010 (http://www.rense.com/general40/closest.htm).

Ian Taylor discusses radio–haloes in basement rocks at length, and they do not support evolution.[26] In Canada, these rocks come to the surface and are known as the Canadian Shield. Microscopically small coloured spheres or haloes found in such rock are the "signatures" of the radioactive products of the uranium–238 decay series. There are fourteen stages of decay of uranium–238, each with a characteristic halo. Some of the original materials are totally missing, so that an age cannot be established. The rocks appear to be created as they are. Therefore, radiocarbon appears useful only for recent timespans. The radio–haloes disqualify all radioactive elements for distant time. Robert Gentry concluded that in 1967.[27] The giant, Science, lost his head.

In 1971, Robert Whitelaw dated the Flood in an article, "Time, Life and History in the Light of 15,000 Radiocarbon Dates."[28] He derived a Carbon–14 production rate variation with time, which in turn led to a correction for the data to the true dates. The figures confirmed his hypothesis of an actual Flood, and the LXX. He came up with 5,000 years ago for the Flood and 7,000 years ago for creation. The giant lost his head again.

The Flood and the ice age came simultaneously, and very suddenly. Some frozen Siberian mammoths still had fresh plants in their stomachs, meaning that they froze very quickly.

---

26 Taylor, Ian. *In the Minds of Men* (Toronto, Canada: TFE, 1984), pp. 309–312.
27 Ibid., p. 312.
28 Whitelaw, Robert L. "Time, Life, and History in the Light of 15,000 Radiocarbon Dates." Creation Research Society Quarterly, 7:56–71.

One specimen was even found aroused—his male organ was still large. An extreme cold had hit him.[29] People apparently ate mammoth meat. In Spain and France, we find paintings of mammoths in caves. Perhaps global warming today still represents the tail end of the ice age?

PRE–FLOOD RIVERHEADS

Roger Waite tells us that when the Bible, in Genesis 2:10, speaks of four riverheads, the Hebrew word used refers to where rivers join together.[30] Ernest Martin first pointed this out.[31]

"In 1996, Boston University scientist Farouk El–Baz examined satellite photos of northern Arabia and Kuwait and to his amazement easily detected a dry riverbed cutting through the limestone of northern Arabia…The bed petered out as it reached the sand dunes of central Arabia." This riverbed fulfills all the requirements for the river Pishon as described in the Bible—we find here gold and precious stones, such as bdellium and onyx. Martin writes, "It fits the description of Havilah." Therefore here was the original site of the Garden of Eden. Here the Tigris and Pishon met.[32] Here were the riverheads. Is there any other scripture like the Bible?

---

29 Taylor, Ian. *In the Minds of Men* (Toronto, Canada: TFE, 1984), pp. 97–100.
30 Waite, Roger. *Mesopotamia in History and Prophecy*, 15 July, 2010, http://www.rogerswebsite.com/graphical, p. 1.
31 Martin, Ernest. *Solving the Riddle of Noah's Flood* (Alexandria, VA: ASK Publications, 1987), pp. 10–11.
32 Waite, Roger. *Mesopotamia in History and Prophecy*. Accessed: 15 July, 2010 (http://www.rogerswebsite.com/graphical).

Early Civilization

The widespread independent testimonies of ancient nations also tell a story. We would expect the memory of a worldwide flood to linger for a long time. As Morris and Whitcomb point out, such accounts would last a few thousand years perhaps, but hardly ten thousands of years or more.[33]

Flood stories have been told all over the world—in China, the Pacific, and Australia. Richard Andree collected and published a number of these accounts in 1891.[34] In Hawaii, Nuhu (obviously a variant of Noah) is the name of the man who saved his family. These stories occur among all races, and import by missionaries does not account for them all.

The best known Flood story outside the Bible is the Gilgamesh epic from Mesopotamia. "Noah and his family migrated to the plain of Shinar, where Nimrod built the city and tower of Babel. Nearby were the cities of Nimrod's kingdom: Babel, Erech, Accad and Calneh. Abraham came from Ur of the Chaldees. We know this area as Sumer, or also as Babylonia."[35]

We find many versions of the creation story outside the Bible. "Eve was known as Nini–ti, the lady of the rib, among the Sumerians. It can also mean 'the lady who causes to live,' which is the epithet that Genesis records of Eve as

---

33 Morris, Henry M. and Whitcomb J.C. Jr. *The Genesis Flood* (Philadelphia, PN: P&R Publishing House, 1966), p. 488.
34 Andree, Richard, *Die Flutsagen*, 1891.
35 Waite, Roger. *Mesopotamia in History and Prophecy*. Accessed: 15 July, 2010 (http://www.rogerswebsite.com/graphical/Mesopotaia), p. 1.

'the mother of all living'...Eden was called Idinu, the paradise in which the 'immortals' lived. Volcano comes from Tubal–Cain, and Cain means blacksmith."[36]

Many reminders of the Bible occur in these accounts. For instance, the Babylonians also have different lists of ten "kings" before the great Flood. Remember, the Bible mentions ten antediluvian patriarchs. A record from Larsa reports the seventh king as Sibzianna. Does his name refer to being the seventh from Adam? The tenth king, Utnapishtum (Xinsuddu, in some records), received warning about a flood, and saved his family by building an ark. But only the Bible places the number ten in a context.

Ten is the number for unregenerate men. In the Bible, it does not say that in so many words, but we have the Ten Commandments, the law for unregenerate men. *"We know that whatever the law says, it says to those who are under the law"* (Romans 3:19, NKJV). The ten horns of the dragon in Revelation 12:3 symbolize the dragon's power over all those who inhabit the earth and the sea, in contrast to the citizens of heaven (Revelation 12:12). The whole world lies in wickedness (1 John 5:19). Nobody does good (Romans 3:10–12). We all need God's grace.

Adam and Eve ate from the tree from which they were not to eat (Genesis 2:17). They then became servants of sin rather than of God to whom they belonged. Romans 6:16 says *"Know ye not, that to whom ye yield yourselves servants*

---

[36] Cooper, Bill. *The Early History of Man, The Table of Nations*. Accessed: 15 July 2010 (http://www.biblebelievers.org.au/).

to obey, his servants ye are to whom ye obey?" (Romans 6:16) They sought a better life, and lost it (John 17:3). They came up short of the Bible's first requirement to love God first of all (Deuteronomy 6:13). God clothed them with skins (Genesis 3:21). They were saved by grace.

The bastard curse lasts for ten generations (Deuteronomy 23:2), and it applies to Adam and Eve, because the bride, God's people (John 3:29), brought forth fruit to Satan. They yielded to him. Because of the curse the human race lasted just ten generations, until the Flood (Genesis 5), but Noah found grace (Genesis 6:8).

Noah sinned. *"So Noah awoke from his wine, and knew what his younger son had done to him"* (Genesis 9:24, NKJV). God had blessed Noah and gave him the rainbow for a sign of it. There were ten generations from Noah to Abraham. This is the context I spoke of.

God did not destroy mankind. He revealed himself to Abraham. God blessed Abraham and destroyed Sodom and Gomorra. To Abraham the promise was renewed. He would be a blessing to the whole earth—*"I will bless those who bless you, and I will curse him who curses you"* (Genesis 12:3, NKJV). Abraham was chosen by grace (Deuteronomy 7:7, 26:5). Everyone saved is saved by grace.

This grace is not the only emphasis in the consideration of the number ten. Another aspect of the bastard curse we see is that Noah sinned, not Shem. Therefore, we start counting the ten generations from Noah, not Shem. If Shem sinned, God does not tell us about it. The ten generations ended with Terah. Abram finds favour, while Sodom and Gomorra are destroyed. Therefore, the second Cainan does not belong there. There is no scriptural warrant for him. We therefore do not consider symmetry or other excuses for his inclusion. This is one reason for the exclusion of Cainan in the genealogy. Here we have a double witness.

To come back to Babylonia, Nimrod, the son of Cush (Genesis 10:8), was the "first Hitler" and the model for all tyrants afterward. The story goes that kingship after the Flood descended down to Kish.[37] Kish, of course, comes from Cush, who was the grandson of Noah (Genesis 10:6). Etana built the very same cities the Bible mentions (Genesis 10:10), and was probably Nimrod. Alexander Heidel showed that Gilgamesh was his name, Nimrod an epithet.[38] Maybe Enmerkar was another epithet. *Nmr* stands for revolt in Hebrew and *kar* for hunter. (*Mercury* is likely related.) In Genesis 10:9, it says of him, *"Even as Nimrod the mighty hunter before the Lord."* He hunted men. A poem of that time says that he had 50 names.[39] Therefore, maybe Etana, Nimrod, Gilgamesh, and Enmerkar are different labels for the same person. There must have been a Nimrod. Ninus is another name for Nimrod, and Nineveh means "dwelling of Ninus."

---

[37] *Enmerkar and the Lord of Aratta.* Accessed: 15 July 2010 (http://www.gatewaystobabylon.com/myths/texts/classic/).
[38] Livingston. David P. "Nimrod: Who Was He? Was He Godly or Evil?" Section: The Gilgamesh Epic. Accessed: 15 July 2010 (http://www.christiananswers.net/dictionary/nimrod.html).
[39] "Enuma Elish: The Babylonian Creation Story." The gods confer kingship on Marduk, hailing him with fifty names. Accessed: 15 July 2010 (http://faculty.gvsu.edu/websterm/Enuma–Elisha.html#1).

Also, the tale of *Enmerkar and the Lord of Aratta* testifies of when people spoke one language: "Once upon a time...the whole universe, the people in unison to Enlil in one tongue gave praise."[40] This mirrors the Bible (Genesis 11:1) very closely.

In short, the Sumerian records confirm the Bible that history starts there. Scripture proves original, and time goes no farther back than creation, about seven thousand years. These are the testimonies from Homo sapiens, not from some race supposed to have evolved millions of years ago. The original writers did not invent their stories to counter today's theory of evolution. The events really happened.

COMMENTARY

God intervened with the Flood and at Babel. Before the Flood, violence filled the earth. *"Now nothing will be restrained from them, which they have imagined to do"* (Genesis 11:6). To restrain sin and man's imagination, God confused their tongues.

Culture descends from the universities, they say, and English has practically become the universal language. History has come full circle, and so has sin. Will God not intervene soon again? 2 Peter 3 tells us that fire will destroy the earth. The lengths of time from creation to the Flood and from Christ until now do not differ much. God has shown patience, not willing that any should perish. God is very good and gave his Son, that whoever puts his trust in him

---

[40] "Enmerkar and the Lord of Aratta." Lines 134–135. Accessed: 15 July 2010 (http:/www.GatewaystoBabylon.com/myths/texts/clas).

should not perish but have eternal life. Accept the offer now! Tomorrow may never come.

Mythology and History

From archaeology we learn that the knowledge of God was quickly lost. After the dispersion of Babylon, the belief in many gods became worldwide. The truth became changed into a lie (Romans 1:25). Out of the trinity became three main gods in many religions. Among the Persians God became the good god and Satan the bad god. Out of the trinity and the angels came a pantheon. In Germanic mythology,[41] and probably among all early groups, God did not create the world; instead it formed out of ice and water in the north and fire in the south. Gods, giants, men, pygmies, and also animals were both ingredients and products of the elements. Men created their own religions.

In *In the Minds of Men*, we read that a thousand years before Moses the literature of Ebla, once an important city, mentions one God.[42] Did the Jews develop monotheism, the belief in only one God? Count it a myth. Melchizedec in Abram's time still worshipped one God. By his mercy, God chose Abram and revealed himself. To the Hebrews God entrusted his oracles.

Nearly two thousand years later, God fulfilled his promise of a Saviour for the whole world. Israel gave birth to a

---

41 Dahn, Felix and Therese. *Walhall* (Kreuznach: Voigtlaender, 1885), p. 17.
42 Taylor, Ian. *In the Minds of Men* (Toronto, Canada: TFE, 1984), pp. 97–100, 389.

spiritual kingdom whose king is Jesus, the Saviour of the world. God revealed himself in him.

Unfortunately, the church added heathen lore to advance itself. The gods of the old religions became the saints of the church—St. Martin, St. George, St. Lionhearted, Madonna. Old heathen feasts became Christian feasts—the midwinter solstice feast became Christmas, the feast of Ostara became Easter, the midsummer solstice feast became the feast of John the Baptist.[43] No wonder then that many look on the Bible as just another collection of myths. Men's understanding was darkened (Romans 1:18–25). Men made evolution a "scientific" religion, in which God is anathema.

Mythmaking continues. Santa Claus replaced Christmas. Reminders that Jesus is the reason for the season may offend some. We may talk about God, but we should not mention Christ. The Bible says that *"men loved darkness rather than light"* (John 3:19), and willingly they are ignorant that God created the world by the Word (2 Peter 3:5). He spoke and the Flood came.

For the sake of political correctness, hospital and army chaplains cannot present Christ. People speak of "Season's Greetings," "Happy Holidays," and even display "holiday trees." The teaching of creation is banned from public schools.

All false doctrine comes under the heading of myth. Even with God's written Word we cannot escape mythmaking except through the Holy Ghost. A study of religions and

---

[43] Dahn, Felix and Therese. *Walhall* (Kreuznach: Voigtlaender, 1885), p. 13.

mythology can make us realize the darkness into which our world has fallen and the blessings of the Scriptures and Christ, who is the light of the world, the bread of life. What a Saviour!

One man was overheard saying, "Look at that, the church is even horning in on Santa Claus."

Photo: The Markdale Standard

Does history presented in Christian education differ from history in public education? Yes, it does. History written without acknowledging God is, in Nebuchadnezzar's words, *"lying and corrupt words,"* the product of imagination (Daniel 2:9). God did give Jehoiakim into Nebuchadnezzar's hand (Daniel 1:2). God dictates history, as made obvious in Daniel 2 and 4, and does not need to resort to fiction. Evolution provides us the lie, and as men choose their ways God will choose their delusions (2 Thessalonians 2:11–12).

In several ways the giant has lost his head. The pride of men—humanism—will never acknowledge it. "Man is the captain of his fate" a humanist will proclaim, but God will assert himself. Christ said, "I am coming soon." His mercy is great, and the door is still open.

Back in History

Genesis 5 follows a strict chronology from creation to the Flood. By the number of years provided for each generation, Genesis 11 also implies a strict order for the genealogy from the Flood to the time of Abraham. There is only one reason to adopt the idea that the list is only a selection of particular men from the genealogy and not the complete list: "We don't believe what the Bible says."

However, fictitious names and the numbers of years would be lies. The Septuagint data fit scripturally and historically. The falling away of the race in four generations—and in four hundred years after the Flood, until Peleg's generation—lines up with the prophecy given to Abraham that the sin of the Amorites was not yet full (Genesis 15:13, 16). Scripturally, we have a double witness—ten generations in each passage.

We established 1871 B.C. as the first year of Hammurabi (see the next chapter, "Abraham"), and we want to trace time back from there. In that year, Rimsin of Larsa overthrew Isin (see next chapter). This history we glean from *Compendium of World History*.[44] The dynasty of Isin goes

---

44 Hoeh, Herman, *Compendium of World History* (1962, Volume 1). Accessed: 3 November 2010 (http://cgca.net/coglinks/wcglit/hoehcompendium/hhc1toc.htm).

back 226 years and ran from the beginning of the reign of Ishbi'erra to the end of that of Damiqilishu. For the start of this dynasty, we come up with 2097 B.C.

Ishbi–Erra's year 15 is year 25 of Ibbi–Sin. Ibbi–Sin was the last ruler of Ur III. He reigned twenty–five years until 2082 B.C. The Nippur king list has dynasties I, II and III of Ur with interruptions and overlaps which cover 542 years (1828–1286 B.C.). That goes back to 2624 B.C., 27 years before Peleg was born.

The compendium has Gilgamesh (Nimrod) become king in Egypt 364 years before the start of Ur I. That would be soon after the Flood. Since here I have lost the timeline, I will not go farther back. This much is certain—we are dealing with true history.

In these essays, several avenues lead to the persuasion that the Greek text is more correct than the Masoretic. Evolution puts on a show of wisdom (Colossians 2:23), but we have the testimonies of people who lived during these times. Evolution says that through death (of the weakest, and survival of the fittest) came man. God's Word says that since by man came death, by man also came the resurrection of the dead (1 Corinthians 15:21). Evolution says there is no God. History shows that God cares. We have the records. In the Septuagint, events fit. It is the scientific way, and God's Word and faith lead the way.

No Cunningly Devised Fables

CHRONOLOGY SUMMARIES

Back from Nebuchadnezzar to the Flood using data from the Bible:

Nebuchadnezzar takes Jerusalem	587 B.C.
Jehoachin's 5th year of captivity	584 B.C.
390 days, 390 years of split kingdom Temple start, 4th year of	975 B.C.
Solomon, rules 40 years	1011 B.C.
From Exodus to the temple start, 440 years, Exodus	1450 B.C.
430 years before the Exodus, Abraham leaves Haran	1880 B.C.
Abraham born in	1955 B.C.

Abraham born 1,042 years after the Flood, Septuagint

The Flood	2998 B.C.

Backward from the battle of the vale of Siddim to the Flood using extrabiblical data:

Battle of the vale of Siddim	1871 B.C.
Fall of Isin	1871 B.C.
Start of Isin dynasty with Ishbi–Erra, 226 years earlier	2097 B.C.
Ishbi–Erra's year 15=year 25 of Ibbi–Sin.	
Ibbi–Sin, last king of Ur III, reigned until	2082 B.C.

Ur I, II, and III were 542 years. Start in	2624 B.C.
Peleg born	2597 B.C.
The Flood	2998 B.C.

Peleg ("division") was so named because the earth was divided soon after he was born. The exact date has not been established. It seems to have occurred in the time of Ur I. By the time his first son was born, Peleg was 130 years old.

THE LAST DAYS

Since we started from the beginning of time, we will also go to the end. In Genesis 49, Jacob tells his sons what will befall them in the last days. He prophesies not just for Israel as a nation, but for spiritual Israel today. Though times may be tough, *"He who overcomes shall inherit all things"* (Revelation 21:7, NKJV; compare this to Matthew 24:13). In Deuteronomy 31:29, Moses tells Israel the same.

Daniel speaks of the latter days and is upset. God, however, comforts him: *"Thou shalt rest, and stand in thy lot at the end of the days"* (Daniel 12:13). God tells Daniel to shut up the words and seal the book to the time of the end, for the time is not yet for many days. The book of Daniel ends with the mention of 1,290 and 1,335 days. That is thirty days more than 1,260—an extension of time, times and a half—and again forty-five days more. In other words, we may think this or that should be the end, but, no, hang in just a bit longer. We see the same in Matthew 10:22 and in Mark 13:8 and 13. "Endure to the end and you will be saved." With this prophecy, God gives a signature, so to speak, just as Paul closed his letters with his own handwriting. For the meaning of 1,260 days and "time, times, and a half," see Chapter Nine, "On Revelation."

In Revelation, the latter times have come. We see the very opposite: *"Seal not the sayings of the prophecy of this book: for the time is at hand"* (Revelation 22:10). Let him who has ears hear what the Spirit says to the churches. Don't add, don't take away. Blessed are those who hear.

Chapter Two

ABRAHAM

Here we show that the event in Genesis 14, when Abraham delivered his nephew Lot from Amraphel, really happened.

Abram left Haran in 1880 B.C., 430 years before the Exodus (Exodus 12:40, LXX). After ten years had passed, Sarai gave Hagar as wife to Abraham (Genesis 16:3). The Bible mentions the battle of the vale of Siddim just before that, so this battle took place perhaps a year before that occasion.

A Wikipedia article about Hammurabi says: "He could have been Amraphel of Shinar in the Jewish records and the Bible."[45] An article on Chedorlaomer by WebBible Encyclopedia–ChristianAnswers Net says, "A recently discovered tablet enumerates among the enemies of Khammu–rabi = Kudur–Lagomar, Eri–Aku of Ellasar (Arioch of Larsa) and

---

45 "First Babylonian Dynasty." Accessed: 3 November 2010 (http://en.wikipedia.org/wiki//First_Babylonian_Dynasty#Origens_of_the_First_Dynasty).

Tudkhula or Tidal."[46] The Bible names the same people; the identification therefore stands.

But why would Hammurabi form a coalition with his enemies? How did Abraham defeat these four allies who had all kinds of victories (Genesis 14:4–11), and how could he have done so with only 318 men? Is this not pure myth? No, Hammurabi got drafted. That same year, Rimsin conquered Isin, which Sinmuballit, Hammurabi's father, had taken just a few years before. Rimsin told Hammurabi, "You are coming with us." Chedorlaomar of Elam was the leader of the coalition (Genesis 14:4–5).

Therefore Abraham may have had an "easy" victory, because Amraphel was not going to stick his neck out for his "friends." Hammurabi maybe even suspected that they wanted to eliminate him before coming back home. Abraham surprised them by night. Nobody knew what was going on, so it was a "save your neck and run" situation. We also read of the enemies of Israel destroying one another in Gideon's time (Judges 7:12 and 22), and in the time of Saul (1 Samuel 14:16, 22).

In the historical records, we have trouble finding any mention of this event. The loser never reported his own defeat, but apparently the defeat was thorough. Silence speaks loudly at times. The Bible talks about the slaughter of Chedorlaomer (Genesis 14:17) and after this event we hear of him no more.

---

46 "Chedorlaomer." Accessed: 3 November 2010 (http://www.christiananswersnet/dictionary/chedorlaomer.html).

Although Hammurabi had to join the campaign, he already proved to be quite independent early in his reign (see extract of year names at end of this chapter.)[47] He published his second year as the "year in which Hammurabi the king established justice/released forced labour in his land." That amounted to abolishing slavery or taxes. That must have built loyalty. He built success. He prepared for war from the beginning. In his fifth year, he made a statue and called it "the lord is the decision maker of heaven and earth." Was this "the lord" a remnant of monotheism? In the seventh year of his reign, Hammurabi seized Isin; any agreement between them had ended. So far it looks like only Hammurabi's first year allows for an alliance.

Rim–Sin (Arioch), in year 15 of his reign, seized Pi–Narratim and Nazarum. The first name suggests a campaign as far as Egypt. (Remember Pi–Ramesse and Pi–Hahiroth?) In those days, the plain of Jordan was *"well watered every where, before the Lord destroyed Sodom and Gomorrah, even as the garden of the Lord, like the land of Egypt"* (Genesis 13:10). In his year 29, Rim–Sin seized Isin and "submitted all the drafted soldiers to his authority" (see extract). This must have happened to Babylon. Genesis 14 tells us about the five kings—*"Twelve years they served Chedorlaomer, and in the thirteenth year they rebelled. And in the fourteenth year came Chedorlaomer, and the kings that were with him"*

---

47 Sigrist, Marcel and Damerow, Peter. "Mesopotamian Year Names, Neo–Sumerian and Old Babylonian Date Formulae." Accessed: 3 November 2010 (http://ca.search.yahoo.com/search;ylt=). "The list is made accessible here as a tool for supporting historical studies. This tool essentially consists of a collection of date formulae for a quick identification of issues and events mentioned in these formulae."

(Genesis 14:4–5)—who defeated a lot of people, including those of Sodom and Gomorrah. These fourteen years were Rim–sin's years 15 through 29. His second campaign came in year 29.

Rim–Sin's year 29b reads, "Year he submitted Isin." Rim–Sin's last year (year 60), reads: "Year 31 he seized Isin." Hammurabi's year 31a reads, in part, "Year Hammurabi the king destroyed the troops of Emutbal and subjugated its king Rim–Sin." So Rim–Sin's 29th year was Hammurabi's first. One scholar asked, "What were they doing that far south? Looking for a battle with Egypt?" I think so. Rim–Sin, after taking Isin, numbered his years from that one event, long after Hammurabi recaptured it.

What conclusions do we draw? In 1871 B.C.—Rim–Sin's year 29 and Hammurabi's year 1—the battle of the vale of Siddim took place. The Bible gives a perfect record. God desires truth in the inward parts, not just a veneer (Psalms 51), and he delivers it.

Neo–Sumerian and Old Babylonian Date Formulae

An Extract from Marcel Sigrist and Peter Damerow.
Rim–Sin of Larsa

15. Year (Rim–Sin) seized with his powerful weapon Pi–narratim and Nazarum.

29a. Year in which Rim–Sin the righteous shepherd, with the help of the mighty strength of An,

Enlil, and Enki, seized in one day Dunnum, the largest city of Isin, and submitted to his orders all the drafted soldiers, but he did not remove the population from its dwelling place.

29b. Year he submitted Isin.

30. Year Rim–Sin the true shepherd with the strong weapon of An, Enlil, and Enki seized Isin, the royal capital and the various villages, but spared the life of its inhabitants, and made great for ever the fame of his kingship.

31. Year after the year he seized Isin/Year 2 (with) the weapon he seized Isin.

32. Year 3 Isin was seized. Until

60. Year 31 he seized Isin.

HAMMURABI OF BABYLON

1. Year Hammu–rabi (became) king.

2. Year in which Hammu–rabi the king established justice/...released forced labour in his land.

3a. Year (Hammurabi) made a magnificent throne dais for the...temple of Nanna in Ur/ the Ekisznugal in Babylon.

3b. Year in which Hammu–rabi built for Nanna his temple in...Babylon.

4. Year in which (Hamu–rabi) restored the great wall of the..."nunnery" and built the great wall of Sziramah/ Isziramah.

5. Year in which (Hammu–rabi) made (a statue called) "the lord...is the decision maker of heaven and earth."

6. Year in which (Hammu–rabi) made a throne for Ninpirig.

7. Year in which (Hammu–rabi) seized Uruk and Isin.

31a Year Hammurabi the king, trusting An and Enlil who...marches in front of his army and with the supreme power...which the great gods have given to him, destroyed the troops...of Emutbal and subjugated its king Rim–Sin and brought...Sumer and Akkad to dwell under his authority.

31b. Year the army of Larsa was smitten by weapons.

Concerning Abraham, there is another sign that the Bible gives us true history and not merely myths. It tells us that Abraham went on to Egypt because there was a severe famine in Canaan. He had instructed Sarah to tell that she was his sister instead of being his wife, because he was afraid that he would be killed on account of her (Genesis 12:9-20). The pharaoh was interested. Who was the pharaoh?

According to Darius Sitek, one man, Malek, published the time of Pepi II's reign as 2236-2143 B.C.[48] Pepi was 100 years old when he died, so that his date of birth was really more like (2243–306) 1937 B.C. (See Chapter 3). Sarah was born in 1945 B.C.(1880 + 65), so that in 1878 B.C. Pepi was 59 years old and Sarah was 67 years old. Given that Sarah gave birth at ninety years old and that she was good-looking, and I suppose young-looking, it would not be unthinkable that he was interested in Sarah as a wife. He was 18 years younger than Abraham.

We are told that one reason that Pepi II was the last main monarch of that dynasty was that the low inundations of the Nile, causing severe droughts between 2200 and 2150 B.C. (1894 and 1844), brought upheaval of agriculture and of government.[49] Time, age, gender and climate agree with the Bible. Nitocris, a queen, reigned after Pepi II for twenty-four years; after that we run into the First Intermediate Period of Egypt.

---

48 Darius Sitek, The VIth Dynasty, http:/www.narmer.pl/dyn/o6en/htm, accessed March 2011.
49 Sir Alan Gardiner, Egypt of the Pharaohs (Oxford: Oxford University Press, 1961), 107.

Chapter Three

ISRAEL IN EGYPT

Blessings Under Joseph

Joseph was Jacob's favourite son by his favourite wife (Jacob had four wives). His father had made him a coat of many colours. Joseph told his brothers his dreams. These dreams offended his brothers even more, so that one day they sold him to traveling traders and he became the servant of Potiphar, captain of pharaoh's guard in Egypt. After faithful service, Joseph ended up in jail, where he interpreted dreams for pharaoh's butler and baker. The butler got his job back but never said a word about Joseph until there came a day when pharaoh wanted to know the meaning of two very strange dreams he'd had. Joseph told pharaoh their meaning. There were coming seven years of bounty and seven others in which the crops would utterly fail. To prepare for the drought, pharaoh appointed Joseph second in command. The full story is found in Genesis 37–41.

After two years of drought, Joseph had his relatives come over to Egypt, where they settled in Goshen (Genesis 45–46) in 1665 B.C. How do we arrive at that year? The Septuagint, the oldest translation of the Jewish scriptures into Greek, tells us that 440 years after the Exodus Solomon started to build the temple (3 Kings 5:18). Because of the double witness, we can show from our Hebrew Bible that this information is correct. (See Chapter Five of this book). Generally, historians accept 966 B.C. as the year of the start of the temple. Ussher knew better, and I take 1011 B.C. (See Chapter Seven.) Because of the preparations under Joseph's directions, the Egyptians and the Hebrews survived the drought.

NOT A MYTH

For a long time, historians considered this story a myth, but we know that this drought really occurred from dendro–chronology, the science of determining wet and dry years from tree rings; the rings vary accordingly. On that basis, Mike Baillie, an Irishman, wrote a book, *Exodus to Arthur*, meaning "from the exodus of Israel out of Egypt until the legendary king Arthur." In it he identifies five very dry periods, one of which ran from 1628 through to 1623 B.C.[50] The Bible gives us 1667 until 1661 B.C.

Many think pharaoh Senusret I appointed Joseph. A German scholar by the name of Brugsch was the first to note

---

50 Zoraster, Steven. A Review of *Exodus to Arthur; Catastrophic Encounters with Comets*, by Mike Baillie. Accessed: 3 November 2010 (http://www.szoraster.com/Science/Exodus%toArthur.htm).

how Senusret had a vizier named Mentuhotep, who was pharaoh's alter ego, an apt ascription of Joseph.[51] Young Senusret inherited his personnel from his father, Amenemhet I, who appointed Joseph in the twelfth year of his reign (see table at end of this chapter). Joseph himself said that God had made him a father to pharaoh (Genesis 45:8). Senusret I had just begun his solo reign at the beginning of the drought.[52] Brugsch decided that the timeframe did not allow for that interpretation, so he missed it.[53]

We learn from a letter of an old farmer to his family that a famine prevailed in the time of Senusret I. An inscription in the tomb of a nomarch at Beni Hassan (governor of a nome, a province), named Amenemhat, or Ameni, refers to famines. He wrote, "No one was unhappy in my days, not even in the years of famine, for I had tilled all the fields in the nome of Mah up to its southern and northern frontiers. Thus I prolonged the life of its inhabitants and preserved the food that it produces. No hungry man was in it. I distributed equally to the widow as to the married woman. I did not prefer the great to the humble in all that I gave away."[54] Ameni probably reminisced about both floods and droughts.

---

51 Brusch–Bey, Henry. *A History of Egypt Under the Pharaohs*, (London, UK: 1879), p. 141.
52 Gardiner, Sir Alan. *Egypt of the Pharaohs*, (London, UK: Oxford University Press, 1964), p. 129.
53 Brusch–Bey, Henry. *A History of Egypt under the Pharaohs*, (London, UK: 1879), p. 137.
54 Ibid, p. 137.

CHANGED TIMES

Exodus 1:8 reads, *"Now there arose up a new king over Egypt, which knew not Joseph."* Until the coming to power of Senusret II in 1576 B.C., Israel dwelt in Egypt almost ninety years. Joseph died nearly twenty years earlier. By then Israel, quadrupling with each generation, would have numbered about 100,000 men. Maybe Senusret II, but certainly Senusret III, promoted infanticide by midwives to the Hebrew women (Exodus 1:15–16, Septuagint). That did not work well. Two midwives could not bring themselves to murder the newborn boys, and God blessed them (Exodus 1:19–21). With a new king came a new order to the whole population to kill the baby boys (Exodus 1:22). The order came in 1532–1531 B.C., just after Aaron was born and just before Moses' birth. Aaron was three years older than Moses (Exodus 7:7). (See chart at end of this chapter.) This order came from Amenemhet III, who reigned from 1535 until 1490 B.C. Egypt also knew a "final solution."

In the nineteenth year of his reign, Amenemhet sent soldiers south,[55] because Ethiopia was taking over the country "as far as Memphis, and the sea itself."[56] The war lasted ten years.[57] The Egyptians consulted their oracles, who advised them to put Moses in command of an army. The Egyptians,

---

[55] Source unknown. See "Leishmaniasis in Ancient Egypt and Upper Nubia." Accessed: 4 November 2010 (http://www.cdc.gov/ncidod/EID/vol12no10/06–0169.htm).
[56] Josephus, *Antiquities of the Jews* (Grand Rapids, MI: Kregal Publications, 1960), Book II, Chapter X. Copyright held by William Whiston.
[57] Rohl, David, *A Test of Time* (London, UK: Century Ltd., 1995), Point 5, p. 301.

who were afraid of Moses, hoped he would be killed in battle; the Hebrews hoped he would deliver them. I used these data, along with others, to adjust the timeframe. See below, under "Biblical Timeframe."

Thermuthis, one of several names for the daughter of pharaoh who had adopted Moses, only let him go because of the desperate situation, and only after a promise that they would not hurt Moses. By good strategy, Moses defeated the Ethiopians and conquered their city of Saba, or Sheba, by promising marriage to an Ethiopian princess.[58] So in the end, Moses saved Egypt. Stephen, in Acts 7:22, most likely referred to this event, saying Moses was mighty in word and deed.[59] The Egyptians would not give credit to a "foreigner." Times had changed. Moses entered the war only when he "came to an age of maturity."[60] The end of the war was in 1506 B.C. By then, Moses was twenty–four years old.

In the days of Amenemhet III, a famine prevailed for nine years. It was not the famine of Joseph's time. This time the Nile subsided too late for a crop.[61] Such a famine would

---

58 Josephus, *Antiquities of the Jews* (Grand Rapids, MI: Kregal Publications, 1960), Book II, Chapter X. Copyright held by William Whiston.
59 Ibid.
60 Ibid.
61 Pope, Charles N., *In the Fulness of Time*. "During the reign of Amenemhet III, disastrously high water levels were recorded at the second cataract in Egypt. To divert some of this excess into the new agricultural district of the Faiyum, and to prevent the Delta from being swamped Amenemhet built great waterwheels. However, beginning with Year 20 the annual waters of the Nile rose to even higher levels. Flood control was overwhelmed and normal planting and harvesting were not possible." See also: Rohl, David. *A Test of Time* (London, UK: Century Ltd., 1995), pp. 407–417.

not show up as a drought in tree rings, nor would it affect Canaan. In Joseph's time, Pharaoh said, *"Seven ears... blasted with the east wind, sprung up"* (Genesis 41:23). Because of the excess water, Amenemhet undertook to drain water into Lake Moeris from the Bahr Yousef, the Joseph canal.[62] In Amenemhat's time also lived a Ptahwer, possibly Potiphar, with a different title than the one in Joseph's time. This famine was too late for Joseph's time. The name Potifera, Joseph's father-in-law (Genesis 41:45), is probably related to Potiphar, and not as rare a name as some suppose. Werner Keller tells us the name means "Gift of God,"[63] very much like John, which is common enough.

Still under Amenemhet III, Moses fled Egypt in 1490 B.C. Forty years later, he returned, when God said, *"Return into Egypt: for all the men are dead which sought thy life"* (Exodus 4:19). Here Moses may have remembered or influenced the story of Sinuhe. For that story, see *The Bible as History*,[64] or look it up on the web.

Amenemhet had no son to succeed him and reigned for a long time. (See chart in this chapter). His daughter, Queen Sebeknefru, ruled after him in the end. Nefrusobek, just another name for Amenemhet's daughter, was barren, and tried to find favour with the gods. Thermuthis (yet another name for pharaoh's daughter) is the Greek form of the Egyptian name Taweret. Taweret refers to the hippopotamus,

---

62 Keller, Werner. *The Bible as History* (Toronto, Canada: George J. McLeod, 1964), p. 86–87.
63 Ibid., p. 86.
64 Ibid., p. 55.

and is the goddess who brings babies to childless women. Sobek (or Sebek) refers to the crocodile, a god of fertility. Pharaoh's daughter also worshipped Hapi, a fertility god of the river. God curses those that curse Abraham (Genesis 12:3) and he cursed Amenemhet. Nowadays, if you belong to Christ, you belong to Abraham (Mark 9:41 and Galatians 3:7). With Amenemhet's death, Egypt broke up and the Second Intermediate Period of Egypt started (See the chapter on the SIP—Egypt's Second Intermediate Period).

"In Llahun, an 'Asiatic' labour camp in the Faiyum, an oasis west of Meidum, many infants died before three months old. They were buried under the floor of the houses in boxes, at times three in a box. Some wore an amulet inscribed with the name of the king in whose time they died. The names started with Senusret II,"[65] who ascended the throne in 1576 B.C., eighteen years after Joseph died. He did not know Joseph (Exodus 1:8). Senusret III knew him even less, because "he came from a different family."[66]

In the plagues before and at the time of the Exodus, God mocked the gods of Egypt (Exodus 10:2, 12:12), and those gods could not save it. "It was plain that the camp had been left in a hurry,[67] even as the book of Exodus tells us. The last king attested was of the 13th dynasty, Neferhotep I,

---

[65] David, Rosalie. *The Pyramid Builders of Ancient Egypt* (London, UK: Guild Publishing, 1986), Plate 16.
[66] Josephus, *Antiquities of the Jews* (Grand Rapids, MI: Kregal Publications, 1960), Book II, Chapter IX, paragraph 1. Copyright held by William Whiston.
[67] David, Rosalie. *The Pyramid Builders of Ancient Egypt* (London, UK: Guild Publishing, 1986), p. 199. Implied on p. 195.

showing that he was probably the king of the Exodus and died in the Red Sea. His burial place is unknown. A brother of his followed him up, Khanefere, Sebekhotep IV."[68]

Biblical Timeframe

Neferhotep died around 1740 B.C. We determine this by subtracting 290 years from 1450 B.C. The data in our chart at the end of this chapter fit even better with 306 years as the difference. The more data we reconcile with each other, the more finely we set our dates; the glove with six fingers belongs to the man with six fingers (2 Samuel 21:20).

God Asserts Himself

Mike Baillie's book ties in the Exodus and its phenomena with the explosion of the island of Thera, present-day Santorini.[69] He supposed that this happened in the seventeenth century B.C., but the Exodus happened in 1450 B.C. Just the same, God did deliver his people with a bang. *"And the Egyptians shall know that I am the Lord"* (Exodus 7:5), and *"Every knee shall bow"* (Romans 14:11, compare Philippians 2:11). We read of these events in the Jewish Midrash, in the Ipuwer papyrus kept in Leiden, and in other texts. Many oral traditions and geographic names witness of them. God will soon take his people out with a bang again (2 Peter 3:10). Be saved! Jesus is the only door.

---

68 Down, David K. "The Chronology of Egypt and Israel." Accessed: 5 November 2010 (http://biblicalstudies.ozwide.net.au/chronology).
69 Zoraster, Steven. *A Review of Exodus to Arthur: Catastrophic Encounters with Comets*, by Mike Baillie. Accessed: 4 November 2010 (http://www.szoraster.com/Science/Exodus%20to%20Arthur.htm)

No Cunningly Devised Fables

Dates as given.[70] (Conventional)	Dates as set by Bible
Amenemhet I reigned from 1991–1962	1685–1656
Joseph sold into Egypt (Genesis 37:12)	1687
Joseph appointed (Genesis 41:46)	1674
Senusret I reigns together with father in 1971	1665
Senusret I reigned from 1962–1917	1656–1611
Drought as per tree rings (1628–1623)	1667–1661
Israel into Egypt	1665
Amenemhet II reigned from 1917–1882	1611–1576
Joseph dies at 110 years old (Genesis 47:9)	1594
Senusret II reigned from 1882–1878	1576–1572
Senusret III reigned from 1878–1841	1572–1535
Amenemhet III reigned from 1841–1796	1535–1490
Aaron is born. (Exodus 7:7)	1533
Order is given to kill infants	1532
Moses is born (Exodus 7:7)	1530
Year 19 of Amenemhet III, soldiers south. In year 29	
Moses saves Egypt	1507
Moses is forty, flees Egypt. (Acts 7:23)	1490
Amenemhet IV reigned from 1796–1790	1490–1484
Queen Sobekneferu reigned from 1790–1786	1484–1480
Moses is 80, Exodus. Neferhotep I dies circa 1740	1450
Sihator, son of Neferhotep, dies circa 1740 (Exodus 12:12)	
Khanefere Sebekhotep IV ruled from 1740–1730	1450–1440

70 Gardiner, Sir Alan. *Egypt of the Pharaohs* (London, UK: Oxford University Press, 1961). The twelfth dynasty dated from 1991–1786 B.C., p. 125.

Chapter Four

HOW MANY PEOPLE IN THE EXODUS?

That God could bring three million people through the desert for forty years, feeding and clothing them, seems too fantastic to believe. It is quite possible, however; it is no myth.

Since Israelites and Amalekites for a whole day fought a variable battle (Exodus 17:8–13), Flinders Petrie, an archaeologist, assumed that the number of Israelites must have equalled the present inhabitants of the Sinai Peninsula. The Amalekites depended on and protected their water sources and mustered all their men. The Sinai most likely supported no more men at that time than it does now. A copyist must not have known that, besides thousand, the word *eleph* also means clan or family group. He saw *eleph* here and *eleph* there and decided to sanitize them. He added them up, and that's how Petrie explained the big numbers. He thought the numbers must have been smaller and he thought he could explain it. Allegedly, the real number was 5,550 men, less than one percent of what the Bible tells us.[71] I doubt that theory.

Problems with Petrie's Assumption

Would the original writer confuse his readers and use one word with two meanings? The first time Scripture gives us any number is in Exodus 12:37. It says that there were about 600,000 men, besides children. Accepting the explanation and reading *clan* instead of *thousand*, we could read that statement as six hundred clans, besides children. That makes no sense. Six hundred clans with less than 6,000 men would give us less than ten men per clan. That makes little sense too. With there being twelve tribes, it could mean less than 500 men for each tribe. The tribes would be very small.

In Numbers 16:49, where 14,700 men died, would that be fifty men per clan (700 divided by 14), while in Numbers 1 there were at most 14 per clan (45,650 Gad)? Moreover, since the whole nation murmured, would just 14 clans be chosen to bear the punishment? Exodus 32:28 poses this same problem. Remember also that the final count varies only a little from the first (Numbers 26). We cannot expect great fluctuations.

Moses's father–in–law advised him to appoint helpers to keep court, because Moses was wearing himself out keeping court day and night, day in and day out (Exodus 18:18). Seventy men helped Moses from then on. Really, were less than 5,500 Israelites that ornery?

---

71 Petrie, Flinders W.M. *Researches in the Sinai*. (London, UK: John Murray, 1906), p. 208.

In Numbers 11:21–23, would Moses have said that the sea would not have enough fish to feed 5,550 men? We can understand it for 600,000 men, but not for 5,550.

There are three hundred short of the total of Levites, but infants one month old would still be quite tender, so that we end up with 22,000 instead of 22,300 (Numbers 3:39). That does not seem too large a difference for that many. The numbers as they are given seem to harmonize. If indeed a copyist made a mistake, was it done ignorantly or deliberately? Either way, did the other scribes just let him do it? All these things work against the assumption.

GROWTH OF JACOB'S IMMEDIATE FAMILY

From age 77 to 130, from the time Jacob left for Paddan–Aram until he stood before Pharaoh, Jacob sprouted into a family of 68 men. Benjamin, born right after the return from Paddan–Aram (Genesis 35:18) and being seven years younger than Joseph (Genesis 30:24–25 and 30:31), had ten sons (Genesis 46:21). Reuben had four sons. Judah and Issachar both had two grandsons. Issachar was born about two years before Joseph. Joseph lived until he was 110 years of age, and saw his grandsons of the third generation (Genesis 50:23). He held Machir's children on his knees. We see four generations in 110 years, almost thirty years for each generation. They thrived. In short, we have good reason to believe the promise that God would multiply Abraham greatly (Genesis 13: 16). Seems like things fit.

215 Years

From the table of dates in the previous chapter, we see that Israel was in Egypt 215 years. Here we confirm it. In Exodus 12:40, we read, *"Now the sojourning of the children of Israel, who dwelt in Egypt, was four hundred and thirty years."* We hear this often. However, our Bible also tells us in Galatians 3:17 that the law came 430 years after the promise to Abraham. The Septuagint is clearer and says that Israel stayed in Egypt and Canaan 430 years. So we should reckon that 430 years passed from the time Abram left Haran.

Dutch BGA[72] gives us a short and precise solution for the time the Israelites dwelt in Egypt. Isaac was born when Abram was hundred years old (Genesis 21:5). That was twenty-five years after he left Haran (Genesis 12:4). Isaac was sixty years old when Jacob was born (Genesis 25:26), and Jacob was 130 years old when he stood before Pharaoh (Genesis 47:9). That leaves 215 years of the 430 years for the time in Egypt.

Here follows an approximation.

- Genesis 29:34–30:25: In 14 years, Jacob begets 11 sons. Levi was about 10 years older than Joseph.

- Genesis 41:46: Joseph appointed—30 years old.

---

[72] Van der Land, J.G. *De Door BGA Verdedigde Chronologie* (Bijbel, Geschiedenis en Archaeologie), http:www.bga.nl/nl/artikelen/chronbga.html.

- Genesis 45:11: Israel entered Egypt—Levi 49 years old.
- Exodus 6:16: Levi dies at the age of 137. He had a son, Kohath. Let's say Levi was age 124 at Jochebed's birth.
- Israel in Egypt 75 years.
- Exodus 6:20: Amram, son of Kohath, weds Jochebed, his aunt!
- Moses born, say, with Jochebed at age 60.
- Israel in Egypt 135 years.
- Exodus 7:7: Moses is 80—Israel in Egypt 215 years.

Although sometimes these figures seem unlikely, we cannot go by today's standard. We also encounter this in the next chapter. In three to four generations, we see God's longsuffering. By then, the sin of the Canaanites had become full (Genesis 15:6).

GROWTH IN EGYPT

How many men could there have been after 215 years? Genesis 46:27 states that all the souls coming into Egypt were 66. Not counting the Levites and Jacob and his sons, that leaves 52 reproductive men. If they quadrupled with each generation (see Genesis 46:8–28 and Exodus 6 for families with four sons, and David Rohl's finding hereafter), it took eight generations to reach over three million men, just counting the last generation. Even with little growth for 80 years, 603,550 men for two generations do not at all seem improbable.

CONTRADICTIONS TO A SMALL NATION

Some try to tell us how small Israel was at the time of the Exodus. That is not quite true. They were only small when they entered Egypt, and especially when God chose Abraham and gave him his oath (Deuteronomy 7:7). We receive confirmation for this in Deuteronomy 10:22: *"Your fathers went down to Egypt with seventy persons, and now the Lord your God has made you as the stars of heaven for multitude"* (NKJV). Deuteronomy 26:5 repeats this: *"My father was a Syrian, about to perish, and he went down to Egypt and dwelt there, few in number; and there he became a nation, great, mighty, and populous."*

That does not refer to 5,550 men. At the Exodus, the situation was different. Exodus 1:7 says that the land was crawling with Israelites. This is not a demagogue saying it. Pharaoh himself admitted that they were more and mightier than the Egyptians (Exodus 1:9). That wouldn't be true if they were less than 6,000 men, or one-thirtieth of that more than two generations back, would it? Did pharaoh need 600 of his best chariots and more for just 6,000 men on foot? (Exodus 14:7, 9)

Dr. Jan Smits

NUMBERS, STATISTICS, AND RATIOS

In Numbers 2, we see the shock troops of Judah in front, since they traveled east. They were the most numerous and strongest, as we may expect (see Luke 14:31). With Petrie's assumption, they would instead only come third in numbers. The northern division comes in second largest; from that direction the Philistines threatened (Exodus 13:17–18). A small group comes at the end, but the very smallest was positioned in the centre. Petrie's assumption bypasses this intelligent arrangement. Instead, we see a beautiful example of how the members take care of each other. The Lord has a purpose in numbers beyond mere information. They tell a story, and here only the bigger numbers make sense.

In Numbers 3, we have 22,273 as the number of firstborn sons of Israel. This gives us the survival rate of sons. If there are 600,000 men from a population with four boys per family, 75,000 should be eldest in the family. So we note a survival rate of only 30%. This agrees with David Rohl's finding that in Avaris the ratio of women to men was about three to one.[73] Here we see the brutal hand of the Egyptians, since this is much higher than a natural mortality rate. No wonder Moses wondered if any of his brethren were still alive (Exodus 4:18). Even so, the Egyptians flouted pharaoh's decree to kill all the baby boys. This again makes sense only for the numbers as given and proves correct our assumption of four boys per family.

---

73 Rohl, David, *A Test of Time*, (London, UK: Century Ltd., 1995), pp. 336–337.

100 sockets, 1 talent each, were used for the boards and posts of the tabernacle, 600,000 *bekahs* made 100 talents, 1 *bekah* per man for a memorial.

Matching Numbers

In Exodus 30:11–16 and 38:25–28, each man paid half a shekel, a *bekah*, quite personally, as a ransom and memorial. For 603,550 men, that amounts to 100 talents and 1,775 shekels. The 100 talents were used for the 100 sockets for the boards and posts of the tabernacle, one talent per socket (see also Exodus 26:15–25, 32 and 36:20–36.) Without the given number of men, they would not reach 100 talents and 1,775 shekels. The silver matched the men. The sockets matched the silver. The boards and posts matched the sockets, two sockets per board. God guarded his honour by a double witness. He is a jealous God (Exodus 20:5). God made it a point: *"For with God nothing shall be impossible"* (Luke 1:37).

NOT KNOWING SCRIPTURE

How do I answer Flinders Petrie? Have faith. He gave God credit for less than one percent. A number of 5,550 men would hardly suffice to hold Jerusalem.[74] Jesus told the Sadducees, *"Ye do err, not knowing the scriptures, nor the power of God"* (Matthew 22:29).

---

[74] Nehemiah 11:1 tells us that 1/10 of the people at the return stayed in Jerusalem. That makes 4,236 (Nehemiah 7:66). *"The city was large and spacious, but the people in it were few"* (Nehemiah 7:4, NKJV). How would that work out with 5,550 men all together?

Chapter Five

FROM EXODUS TO TEMPLE

In 1450 B.C., Israel left Egypt. The Septuagint reads that Solomon began the temple in the 440th year after the Exodus (3 Kings 5:17, Septuagint). The King James, in 1 Kings 6:1, says it was 480 years. The versions clash. God's Word does not easily come apart, and by the double witness we want to check this out. The building of the temple began in 1011 B.C. (See next chapter.)

First step

Caleb was forty years old when he spied out the land one year after the Exodus (Joshua 14:7). He was 85 when Joshua subdued the land, and still felt fit for battle (Joshua 14:10). This was 46 years after the Exodus. The Bible never calls Caleb stricken with old age, unlike Joshua (Joshua 13:1). Joshua does not lead any more campaigns, but sends people out. Joshua dies at the age of 110 (Joshua 24:29). Six years earlier, Moses had died at the age of 120. Joshua, the son of Nun, is called a young man in Exodus 33:11, when the Israelites were still at Horeb, so that he was about thirty years younger than Moses. He then must have been about eleven years older than Caleb. Judges 2:7 reads, *"And the people served the Lord all the days of Joshua, and all the days of the elders that outlived Joshua, who had seen all the great works of the Lord, that he did for Israel."* At the time of Joshua's death, Israel had lived in Canaan twenty years. Another twenty years would dull the impact of history and the memory of God. Therefore:

Let's count for Joshua and elders	37 years
According to Judges,	
we have Chushan–rishathaim	8
Rest under Othniel	40
Moab, Eglon with	(18)
Ehud, Shamgar	80
with Jabin	(20)
Rest under Deborah and Barak	40
Midian	7
Rest during Gideon	40
Abimelech	3
Tola	23
Jair	22
Ammonites	(18)

That gives us Jephthah's total of 300 years from 1410 B.C.

Consider that Ehud did not live 80 years after his victory; only the land had rest that long. However, after his death Jabin oppressed Israel twenty years. In the song of Deborah we read "In the days of Shamgar" (Judges 5:6). In the Second Step we will see that oppression is not quite the same as serving someone. Rather, it is more like being vexed. Jabin, Moab and Ammon oppressed Israel, or occupied only part of it. Here again, if part suffers, the whole suffers. I did not count in those years.

SECOND STEP

Now that we have seen how the biblical data may fit together for the first 340 years following the Exodus, we want to see how events fit together for the final 100 years, supposing that 440 years passed from the Exodus until the start of the temple.

From the start of Jephthah's reign to the end of the Philistine oppression, 71 years passed—31 years plus 40 (Judges 12:7 to 13:1).

That means that, from the end of the oppression until the start of the temple, there were 29 years, which brings us 15 years into David's reign from Hebron, or eight years since the start of his reign in Jerusalem. We don't need to try with 140 years. Josephus confirms Saul's twenty years.[75] Luke, in Acts 13, writes what Gamaliel had taught Paul.

The forty years of oppression end at 2 Samuel 8:1. It says there that David smote and subdued the Philistines, and took Metheg–Ammah out of their hands. The Philistines lost their Bridle of Ammah, their hold on Israel. David was

[75] Josephus, *Antiquities of the Jews* (Grand Rapids, MI: Kregal Publications, 1960), Book VI, Chapter XIV, Verse 9. Copyright held by William Whiston.

45 years old. The Bible, in 1 Chronicles 18:1, tells us that David took Gath. This happened before Solomon was born, who became king when David was seventy. As in the first step, we cannot just add up the given figures. The oppression was during the reigns of Saul and David.

The Philistine oppression started five years before Saul's reign (15 years for David, plus 20 years for Saul out of a total of 40 years). Samuel was told to anoint Saul *"captain over my people Israel, that he may save my people out of the hand of the Philistines: for I have looked upon my people, because their cry is come unto me"* (1 Samuel 9:16). Saul had his first battle with them and died fighting them. The oppression lasted forty years, and Saul reigned only 20 years. It remained for David to finish the job. In 2 Samuel 3:18, we read, *"By the hand of my servant David I will save my people Israel out of the hand of the Philistines."* 2 Samuel 5:17 tells us that the Philistines fought with David as soon as he became king of all Israel.

The assumption that Samuel brought back the ark after twenty years includes the assumption that Israel lost it before Saul's days. The Bible does not mention a word about Samuel bringing back the ark, but when David brought it back they sure celebrated (2 Samuel 6:12–19).

I will add one more proof that the time from the Exodus to the beginning of the temple construction was 440 and not 480 years. David became king at thirty years of age (2 Samuel 5:4). The time between the entry into Canaan and the birth of David equals 325 years (1410 years minus 1085). Boaz was born of Salmon and Rahab (Matthew 1:5) no later than fifty years after the entry into Canaan. Rahab then would at least be 70. That leaves 275 years, or 92 years each for Boaz, Obed, and Jesse to beget a son. Note that we reckoned with 440 years. With 480 years in between, that would instead mean 105 years each to father a son (40 divided by 3 makes 13 years more for each). And the Bible would not record such a series of miracles?

We see then that the Masoretic text has been tampered with, and sometimes the Septuagint is right. God watches over his Word and always gives a double witness. *"The zeal of the Lord of hosts will perform this"* (Isaiah 9:7).

CHANGED PERSPECTIVES

Since David fetched the ark back after twenty years, in his first year at Jerusalem, and Saul reigned 20 years, the Philistines captured the ark seven to eight years into Saul's reign. David had reigned seven to eight years in Hebron. We tend to think that Israel lost the ark long before Saul's reign, but we need to straighten out the chronology in 1 Samuel.

In 1 Samuel 3, Eli gets the second notice of doom for his family. According to Genesis 41:32, the prophecy must come to pass. 1 Samuel 3 really ends halfway verse 4:1, where the word of Samuel came to all Israel. The story picks up again in 7:3. Since the word of the Lord came to Samuel, he starts preaching and teaching: *"If ye do return unto the Lord with all your hearts, then put away the strange gods"* (1 Samuel 7:3). A revival starts. The children of Israel put away the gods of Baalim and Astaroth. Samuel then interceded for Israel, and God heard. Israel won the battle. After the battle at Mizpeh, Samuel puts up his Ebenezer (meaning "this far the Lord has brought us"). I Samuel 7:13 says, *"So the Philistines were subdued, and they came no more into the coasts of Israel: and the hand of the Lord was against the Philistines all the days of Samuel."*

Samuel first calls the place Eben–Hezer in I Samuel 7:12. That story, going by order of events, therefore should come before 4:7, where Israel pitched beside Ebenezer. In I Samuel 14:18, the ark was still with Israel, having never left it. In 14:3, we read that Ahiah, also known as Ahimelech (Ichabod's uncle) was there. Eli is designated as the priest in Shiloh; he was still living. Samuel, on this occasion, arrived just to take off again. The author/editor, whoever tried to straighten out the story, speaks of Ichabod to identify Ahiah, since he already mentioned Ichabod. Ichabod was not born until after the ark was lost to the Philistines. In I Samuel 15, we have the final break of God with Saul; Israel had the victory, but Samuel came no more to see Saul. The days of Samuel had ended.

I Samuel 13:1 says, *"Saul reigned one year; and when he had reigned two years over Israel..."* It makes no sense. Verse 8 states, *"And he tarried seven days, according to the set time that Samuel had appointed [set]."* This arrangement had been made in I Samuel 10:8. Saul was still to become king. Where is the saying of how old Saul was and how long he reigned? This is the place for it. In 2 Samuel 3:10 and 2 Samuel 5:4, such statements are made. They are parallel passages. Here the line clearly has been corrupted. In the original, it may have run like this: "Saul the son of Kish was 44 years old when he became king, and he reigned over Israel 20 years." In the New American Standard Bible, the verse runs somewhat like that. The first thing Saul did, he failed at; he could not wait a full seven days. He did not disobey two years later. Note that Jonathan's armour bearer was a young man (I Samuel 13:6), so Saul must have been in his forties.

In I Samuel 14, we do not see the ark on the battlefield. King Saul only was thinking about getting the ark. The ark was lost to the Philistines in Chapter 4 to 7:3, after Saul had reigned seven years. We read that never before such a thing was heard of. When Saul said, in 14:19, Withdraw your hand, it meant as much as "forbear, don't bother." The story of the loss of the ark should come just before Chapter 16. Samuel mourned over Saul. He had anointed him, and after the loss of the ark must have sat down for a talk with the Lord. In I Samuel 16 the Lord told him that He was through with Saul. He told Samuel to go and anoint a son of Jesse.

So, Samuel anointed David, and Saul persecuted David for twelve to thirteen years. David became king at Hebron at age 30. Ishbaal, forty years old, succeeded Saul (2 Samuel 2:10).

Because of Ishbaal's age, it is easy to assume that Saul reigned forty years. However, when Saul began to reign Ishbosheth was not mentioned (I Samuel 14:49), because he was Ishbaal, a man of Baal. Ishbosheth, his other name, means "man of shame." Don't forget what Saul called Jonathan (I Samuel 20:30). Saul did not die on the battlefield in his eighties, but in his sixties. In Saul's reign, Ichabod, meaning "the Glory has departed," was born. David in his sixties was urged to keep out of battle (2 Samuel 21:15–17). Abishag could not comfort him when he was seventy (1 Kings 1:4).

Eli was 98 when he died, and had judged Israel for 40 years (1 Samuel 4:18). Samuel was about six when he came to Eli, after he was weaned. Eli had grown sons who had made history already; Eli was 46–48 years old then. If Eli had judged Israel for 40 years at 98, he must have begun when Samuel was 16. Whereas in Shiloh, at first, *"the word of the Lord was precious"* (1 Samuel 3:1), later on *"the Lord revealed himself to Samuel"* (1 Samuel 3:21).

The forty years of servitude mentioned in Judges 13:1 are overlapped by Eli, Samuel, and Samson. Eli died when Israel lost the ark. Since David went to Paran after Samuel died (1 Samuel 25:1) and David was with Achish for one year and four months (1 Samuel 27:7), Samuel must have died about two years before Saul died. (See endnote 68.) He was 68 years old. Although we tend to think that in those days people became very old, this is really only the exception. It is Moses in Psalms 90:10, not David, who says, *"The days of our years are threescore and ten; and by reason of strength they be fourscore years."* Of Samson, we know that he was born at the beginning of the oppression and judged Israel for twenty years. He died just before David took Metheg–Ammah, or Gath, and thus contributed to the victory.

Spring of 1945. Liberation is here!
Apeldoorn. Great joy!

The end of World War II, celebration of
V-E Day in Toronto.

City of Toronto Archives, Fonds 1266, Item 96241

Dr. Jan Smits

"This is my body broken for you. This cup is the new testament in my blood. This do in remembrance of me."

"That which was glorious had no glory, because of the glory that excels" 2 Corinthians 3:10.

The Last Supper, by Dieric Bouts,
1419–1475, Leuven.

CHAPTER SIX

EGYPT'S SECOND INTERMEDIATE PERIOD

Egypt boasts one of the world's oldest civilizations. Israel resided there and, being a neighbour, its history closely intertwines with Egypt's. Discussing this history will illustrate and confirm some of my points. Greenberg, on his website, *Bible, Myth and History*, admits, "The presently accepted view of Egyptologists is that the first dynasty began no earlier than about 3100 B.C."[76] That comes close to what we obtain biblically. Because scientists in general regard the Bible as myth, in history they ignore God, but *"the stone which the builders refused is become the head stone of the corner"* (Psalms 118:22). As I said earlier, God's Word and faith lead the way. The SIP, Egypt's Second Intermediate Period, runs from the end of the reign of queen Sobeknefru, 1480 B.C. (see list of dates at the end of Chapter Three), to the New Kingdom. It might be called the Second Dark Age, because events are very confused.

---

76   Greenberg, Gary. "Bible, Myth and History, Manetho's Chronology." Accessed: 5 November 2010 (http://www.ggreenberg.tripod.com).

Dr. Jan Smits

Problems with Sothic Dating

Sothic dating is tied to Sirius, the dog star. Sothic dating has the period lasting from 1786 B.C. to 1575 B.C., in total 211 years. It obviously frustrated Sir Alan Gardiner, but by and large historians still honour his dictum when he wrote, "To abandon 1786 B.C. as the year when Dynasty XII ended would be to cast adrift from the only firm anchor, a course that would have serious consequences for history, not of Egypt alone, but of the entire Middle East."[77] He observed that "Manetho too regarded his dynasties as consecutive. "The alternative, which all Egyptologists accept, is that the canon's enumeration comprised many kings existing simultaneously, but presumably in widely distant parts of the country." He further observed that "Unhappily, it is only seldom that a king of the Turin list can be pinned down to a restricted area," but never mind the canon or Manetho, the historians liked the myth. It reminds me of a joke. This fellow meets his neighbour at night, drunk, under a lantern looking for his keys. He asks, "Did you lose them here?" The neighbour answers, "No, I don't think so, but here I get some light."

Various authors differ on the time of the SIP and exceed the number of 211 years. Ryholt defines the Second Intermediate Period as the timespan between Sobeknefru and Dynasty 18.[78]

According to Gardiner, The Turin Canon, the Saqqara king

---
77 Gardiner, Sir Alan. *Egypt of the Pharaohs* (London, UK: Oxford University Press, 1964), p. 148.
78 Ryholt. K.S.B. *The Political Situation in Egypt During the Second Intermediate Period* (Copenhagen, Denmark: Museum Tusculanum Press, CNI Publications, 1997), p 1. On page five, he says that the 14th dynasty ushered in the SIP and lasted until the Hyksos conquered Avaris.

list, and Manetho are unanimous on the point.[79]

Ryholt has it last from circa 1800 B.C. until circa 1550 B.C. Janine Bourriau defines the SIP as the "division of Egypt," beginning much later and ending at the fall of Avaris in circa 1550 B.C. The fall of Avaris comes "between years 18 and 22 of Ahmose," more or less twenty years past the start of the New Kingdom.[80]

A DIFFERENT OPINION

Solomon started building the temple at Jerusalem 440 years after Israel left Egypt (3 Kings 6:1, Septuagint). The SIP started and ended sooner than that, but should have lasted about the same length of time.

Gardiner, discussing the Turin list, recognizes, "Indubitably the Rameside compiler believed himself able to present the hundred or so kings known to him in a single continuous series, with the exact length of each reign correctly stated. The number of years is preserved in some twenty–nine cases, these totaling in all 153 years."[81] So, if one third of the kings took 153 years, the whole number of kings could have taken three times as long.

Someone else disagrees. "Hall wrote that the evidence of linguistic and cultural change would require it to be 400 or 500 years in extent. On the other hand, Velikovsky restored

---

79 Gardiner, Sir Alan. *Egypt of the Pharaohs* (New York, NY: Oxford University Press, 1961), p. 148.
80 Bourriau, Janine, *The Oxford History of Ancient Egypt* (Oxford, UK: Oxford University Press, 2000), p. 185.
81 Gardiner, Sir Alan, *Egypt of the Pharaohs* (New York, NY: Oxford University Press, 1961), p. 148.

the Manethonian duration for the Hyksos period[82] in place of the 100 years to which modern chronology reduces it. According to authorities he quoted, there are many cultural considerations indicating a period much longer than the 100 years for the SIP, but the tyranny of Sothis dating forced modern historians to ignore them. Petrie even proposed an additional Sothis cycle—1460 years—between them."[83]

Manetho, an Egyptian priest, wrote an Egyptian history. His works are lost, but Africanus, Eusebius and Josephus, whose works still exist, quoted him. They contradicted each other. Gary Greenberg claims to reconcile the contradictions and rehabilitate Manetho.[84] He does a bit, but again he has too many kings for the allotted time. Also because of Sothic error, he runs about 306 years early (see Chapter Three, "Biblical Timeframe").

Both Africanus and Eusebius have Dynasty 13 lasting 453 years. Gary Greenberg recognized this as the sum of all five dynasties of the period.[85] Africanus and Eusebius mistook Manetho; Greenberg did not misunderstand, but chose the consensus, the wide gate in the parable (Matthew 7:13).

Both Africanus and Eusebius say that Dynasty XIV (ours XIII) lasted 184 years; 86 hence, Manetho likely said so.

82 Don Mills, in a Wikipedia discussion, July 1999. He quotes Josephus, *Against Apion* (Grand Rapids, MI: Kregal Publications, 1960), Book I, p. 84. Apparently on page 26, Manetho mentions that Thutmose was king when the Hyksos left Egypt after 518 years. See also Book I, p. 31.
83 Don Mills in a Wikipedia discussion, July 1999.
84 Greenberg, Gary. "Bible, Myth and History, Manetho's Chronology." Accessed: 5 November 2010 (http://www.ggreenberg.tripod.com). From discussions in Egyptology #25, Table 2.
85 Ibid.

No Cunningly Devised Fables

Dynasty XIV (ours, theirs XIII) began in 1490 B.C., at the death of Amenemhet III (see list at end of Chapter Three) and lasted 194 years. We should consider 184 years as a true unit in history. I conclude that in 1296 B.C. the Hyksos made Avaris their capital. Since I do not believe that Manetho wrote three books of history just to impress the Greeks with the antiquity of Egypt, for all these reasons I believe that 453 years for the SIP should not be far off the mark. Moreover, Ryholt admits that the heading on the Turin king list (designated location 7/4) may stand for the entire SIP.[86] This he admits in spite of claiming that "the corrupt and unreliable Manethonian tradition" has long obstructed the study of the SIP.[87]

The Start of the New Kingdom

Though various authors define the start of the SIP differently, most agree that it ended with the New Kingdom. When did the New Kingdom start?

2 Chronicles 8:1 states that at the end of twenty years, Solomon (1015–975 B.C) had built the house of the Lord and his own house. In 9:1, a bit later, the queen of Sheba came to Jerusalem to prove him with hard questions. Solomon had married an Egyptian princess, and therefore he belonged to the family (2 Chronicles 8:11).

In Matthew 12:42, Jesus calls the queen of Sheba *"the queen of the south."* Josephus calls her the queen of Egypt and

---

86 Ibid., p. 33, note 83.
87 Ibid., p. 2.

Ethiopia.[88] David K. Down gives reasons for Queen Hatshepsut's trip to the land of Punt being to Judah (2 Chronicles 9:10–12).[89] She would be the illustrious visitor. She called it the land of God. Scripture tells us *"there was no more spirit in her"* (1 Kings 10:5). The glory overwhelmed her; she had a taste of heaven.

Thutmose III, Hatshepsut's nephew who reigned right after her, plundered Jerusalem in Rehoboam's fifth year (1 Kings 14:25–26). Rehoboam succeeded Solomon, so the year was 971 B.C. This was year 22 of Thutmose's reign,[90] meaning he ascended the throne in 994 B.C. He sacked Jerusalem 23 years after the visit!

Going back from Thutmose III and the visit of Hatshepsut, the New Kingdom started in 1051 B.C. (See the next chart.) The SIP, as defined, lasted 429 years. The histories of Egypt and Israel agree perfectly.

	Dates B.C. set by Bible	Length of reign (Web)
Ahmose I	1051–1028	24 (start of New Kingdom)
Amenhotep I	1027–1007	21
Thutmose I	1006–995	12
Thutmose II	994–993	2
Hatshepsut	992–971	22
Thutmose III	992–939	54

88 Josephus, *Antiquities of the Jews* (Grand Rapids, MI: Kregal Publications, 1960), Book II, Chapter VI. Copyright held by William Whiston.
89 Down, David K. "The Chronology of Egypt and Israel." Accessed: 5 November 2010 (http://biblicalstudies.ozwide.net.au/chronology).
90 "Thutmose III." Accessed: 6 November 2010 (http://wikipedia.org/wiki/Thutmose_III).

However, the five dynasties cover more than the SIP as defined. Dynasty 14 started ten years before, and Dynasty 17 ran into Dynasty 18 by fourteen years. Ahmose, founder of Dynasty 18, began the re-conquest of the Hyksos starting around the eleventh year of his reign.[91] He was about twenty-one years old at the fall of Havaris. That gives us 453 years, exactly as Manetho said and Greenberg recognized. Their time ran from 1490 to 1037 B.C. Manetho must have defined the SIP the same way Bourriau did—"the division of Egypt." Only, the division he had in mind was earlier.

Now, Velikovsky has argued that the Amalekites were the Hyksos. That may be so. Saul defeated the Amalekites maybe five years into his reign, that would make it ca. 1070 B.C. It says in 1 Samuel 15:7, *And Saul smote the Amalekites from Havilah until thou comest to Shur, that is over against Egypt.* The fall of Avaris after a three year siege was in 1037 B.C.

ANOTHER LOOK AT DYNASTY 14

The Bible does not indicate great turmoil in Egypt during Moses' absence. Exodus 2:23 says that in the process of time, the king of Egypt died, and that *"all the men are dead which sought thy life"* (Exodus 4:19). Moses by then had dwelt in Midian forty years. Some Egyptologists have concluded the same. Rosalie David said, "It seems like the takeover was not too chaotic" and "for more than a hundred years the central government continued."[92]

---

91 "Ahmose." Cambridge Encyclopedia, Third Volume (http://encyclopedia.stateuniversity.com/pages/744/Ahmose_I.html).
92 David, Rosalie. *The Pyramid Builders of Ancient Egypt* (London, UK: Guild Publishing, 1986), pp. 197–198.

Dynasty 14 did not start with Nehesy. The Turin king list shows Nehesi as the second king of Dynasty 14.[93] That makes Sheshi, his father, first, which agrees with the Bible. No other king in Dynasty 14 reigned forty years.[94] On his website, called *14th Dynasty*, Kinnaer, a Belgian Egyptologist, says that "this dynasty seems to have had good relationships with Nubia and at least one of its kings, Sheshi, may have been married to a Nubian princess."[95]

Jacques Kinnaer writes that, although there was war between them at first, after a while Dynasty 13 and Dynasty 14 even allowed each other trade in their territories.[96] He also writes, "The second part of the 13th dynasty, however, was marked by usurpations, and kings openly proclaiming their non–royal birth. At the same time the kings of the 14th dynasty became more and more ephemeral figures." Rather, a glance at the king list shows us that from the beginning Dynasty 13 changed more often than those in Dynasty 14. That and the common threat from the Hyksos may have contributed to the peace between them.

Jacques Kinnaer says, "Remarkably, several kings of the 14th dynasty had the word *nourishment* as part of their royal

---

93 Sitek, Darius. "Ancient Egypt: History & Chronology XIVth dynasty, c.1710–c. 1590." Accessed: 6 November 2010 (http:/narmer.pl/indexen.htm).
94 Ryholt, K.S. B. *The Political Situation in Egypt During the Second Intermediate Period* (Copenhagen, Denmark: Museum Tusculanum Press, CNI Publications, 1997), Note 903.
95 Ibid., pp. 46–48. "Nehsy can be shown to be the son and successor of king Sheshi." (Bietak SAK 11, 71–72).
96 Kinnaer, Jacques. "The Ancient Egypt Site, 2nd Intermediate Period (1783–1540)." Accessed: 6 November 2010 (http://ancient–egypt.org/).

names, an indication that the provision of food became a topic of high political importance. At the same time, burials in Avaris, the capital of the 14th dynasty, often lacked the usual food offerings and have the character of quick mass interments." We see "a quick succession of kings in both dynasties." Ryholt's king list of the dynasty shows these short reigns clearly after Sheshi[97] and we have another reason to believe that Sheshi was the pharaoh while Moses was in Midian. Shortly after his reign came the Exodus. Egypt was destabilized. Ryholt discusses these matters in his book (p. 300).

Sheshi founded the dynasty. The five kings that Ryholt assumes belonged in the lacuna at the start of Dynasty 14 do not belong there. (A lacuna, in this context, is a gap of kings reported in the *Vorlage*.) There was no lacuna. Sheshi's successors were ephemeral and Moses and Aaron dealt with Nehesy.

Ryholt admits the possibility of only one missing pharaoh. "Column 8 can be estimated originally to have contained 29 lines and therefore just two lines are entirely lost at the bottom. This would leave room both for a summation of the Thirteenth Dynasty and a heading for the Fourteenth dynasty which follows in column 9… We thus have three possibilities."[98] The possibility he chooses is highly speculative: there is not just something missing, but also a sign for a lacuna in the *Vorlage* (what the list is copied from). The lacuna was for five kings, and

---

97 Ryholt, K.S.B. *The Political Situation in Egypt During the Second Intermediate Period* (Copenhagen, Denmark: Museum Tusculanum Press, CNI Publications, 1997), Table 95, Kings 5 and 6, p. 409.
98 Ibid., pp. 69–70.

the sign for the lacuna disappeared. He places too much faith in the seriation of royal scarab seals, the arranging of seals in series in order to determine chronology.

In Exodus 9:14, we read, "I will... send all my plagues... that thou mayest know that there is none like me in all the earth." The Exodus, with its plagues, left the country devastated; the signs are there. Sheshi's immediate successor, Nehesy, reigned solo for less than a year, and qualifies more as pharaoh of the Exodus than Neferhotep of Dynasty 13. He drowned in the sea.

Ryholt states, "Two archaeological contexts make it clear that both Sheshi and Ya'qub–Har must be dated well before the Hyksos age. A seal impression of Sheshi was found at the Uronarti fortress in Nubia... which can with some certainty be dated to the early Thirteenth Dynasty."[99] Also he tells us that "a seal impression of Sheshi was found at the Mirgissa fortress, which Neferhotep abandoned."[100] Cartouches found at El–Lahun attest that Neferhotep and Sheshi were indeed contemporaries.

We already concluded that Amenemhet III died in 1490 B.C., the year Moses fled. Amenemhet IV, also known as Khenefre, took over. Although Dynasty 14 started ten years earlier, Dynasty 13 was considered the more legitimate of the two, but Scripture actually recognizes Sheshi as the king of Egypt (Exodus 2:23, 3:10, and on). Paul writes that Jannes

---

99 Ibid., p. 42, last paragraph.
100 Ibid., Note 111.

and Jambres withstood Moses (2 Timothy 3:8). The name Jambres is probably a form of Chenefres or Khenefre.

In passing, note that I said Amenemhet IV (Khenefre) took over. This illustrates what Gardiner remarks, that the rulers of Dynasty 13 "desperately clung to the hope of being recognized as legitimate successors of Dynasty XII."[101] Artapanus wrote that Merris married Khenefre.[102] This was her husband, not the Khenefre who ruled after the Exodus. Moses, at the time of the Exodus, was 80 years old—Nefrusobek was at least 100. Her husband was Amenemhet IV, an earlier Khenefre. Jacques Kinnaer tells us that her husband did not belong to the royal family.[103] Sobekhotep IV later used the name (after all, Amenemhet IV was a pharaoh) to profess legitimacy. Some had royal blood while others gloried in being of the people. By using the name Khenefre, Sobekhotep IV may have appealed to both sides.

Daphna Ben Tor and James and Susan Allen, in a book review, BASOR 315, level an interesting criticism at Ryholt's assumption that Dynasties 13 and 14 were pretty well concurrent.[104] They "conclusively establish that the 14th dynasty was only contemporary with the 13th dynasty in the last half-century of the latter's existence." Also, "Manfred

---

101 Gardiner, Sir Alan. *Egypt of the Pharaohs* (London, UK: Oxford University Press, 1961).
102 Artapanus mentioned in Praeparatio Evangelica (Eusebius 9:27.3).
103 Kinnaer, Jacques. "The Ancient Egypt Site, 2nd Intermediate Period (1783–1540), 14th dynasty." Accessed: 6 November 2010 (http://ancient–egypt.org/), first line.
104 BASOR stands for Bulletin of the American Society for Oriental Research. Issue 315 was released in 1999, pp. 47–73.

Bietak has dated the inscriptions and monuments of Nehesy at Tell el–Dab'a in the delta—the first known Dynasty 14 king—to stratum F or B/3 of the Bronze Age at around 1700 B.C.—corresponding to the late 13th dynasty."[105]

It is interesting because they are all somewhat right. Ryholt, by having Dynasty 14 start with Yakbim Sekhaenre (see his chronological table 95[106]), places Nehsy a whole century later than the dynasty started. In reality, Nehsy came forty years after the start of the dynasty. Remember the three blind men describing an elephant? Each feels a different part and, of course, they disagree in their conclusions.

This new understanding about Ancient Egypt creates all kinds of puzzles for Egyptologists, but in conclusion, the Bible is a boon to archaeology, and history. We often see that it is not a matter of history supporting the Bible, but rather the reverse. David Rohl came to realize this. His book, *A Test of Time*, carries the subtitle *The Bible, from Myth to History*.[107] Science still needs to catch up with the Bible. The Word of God is authoritative. Let us therefore not entertain a slave mentality that wants to go "back to Egypt," but in full assurance let us take encouragement from the Scriptures (Romans 15:4 and 1 Corinthians 10:11).

---

105 Bourriau, Janine. *The Second Intermediate Period, The Oxford History of Ancient Egypt* (Oxford, UK: Oxford University Press, 2002), pp. 178–1279, 181.

106 Ryholt, K.S. B. *The Political Situation in Egypt During the Second Intermediate Period* (Copenhagen, Denmark: Museum Tusculanum Press, 1997), p. 409.

107 Rohl, David, *A Test of Time: The Bible as History*, (London, UK: Century Ltd., 1995).

Chapter Seven

SOLOMON'S TEMPLE AND THE DIVIDED KINGDOM

The purpose of this chapter is to establish and confirm when Solomon started to reign and when he began to build the temple.

Historians established the start of the temple by Solomon at 966 B.C. I assumed they had that right. Bishop James Ussher knew better. He used the Bible, and I stand corrected. I will use 586 B.C., the destruction of Jerusalem,[108] as my starting point.

Nebuchadnezzar ascended the throne in August or September after the death of his father, Nabopolassar. Astronomy confirms the years of his reign.[109] His accession was in 605 B.C. His first year (604 B.C.) was the fourth for Jehoiakim

---

108 Ussher, James. *The Annals of the World,* revised and updated by Larry and Marion Pierce (Green Forest, AR: Masterbooks, 2003), p. 104.
109 Feuerbacher, Alan. "Part 2: Discussion of Historical Evidence" (especially of VAT 4956). Accessed: 6 November 2010 (http://corior.blogspot.com/2006/02/part–2–discussion–of–historical.html#astro).

(Daniel 1:1). In his eighth year, 597 B.C, Jehoiakim's eleventh, he captured Jerusalem and set up Zedekiah (2 Chronicles 36:5, 10). In 587 B.C., Zedekiah's eleventh year, Jerusalem fell again (2 Chronicles 36:11) and early in the year 586 B.C. Nebuchadnezzar's men destroyed the city.

Daniel became a captive at the first siege of Jerusalem in 605 B.C. King Cyrus in his first year allowed the Jews to go back to Jerusalem (536 B.C.) At first, only some people were carried away, but the Bible uses these dates to place the Babylonian exile. After the Exodus in the desert, the stronger tribes took care of the weaker ones; here again we see that if one member suffers, the whole body suffers.

Ezekiel, in the fifth year of the captivity of Jehoiachin (Ezekiel 1:2), received orders to illustrate the sin of the northern tribes for 390 years by lying on his left side for 390 days (Ezekiel 4:5, 593 B.C.). The sign, with Jerusalem portrayed as besieged, amounted to a short–term prophecy to confirm Ezekiel as a prophet (Jeremiah 28). Jerusalem was doomed. In Ezekiel 24:2, the prophecy was confirmed. In Ezekiel 33:21, the twelfth year of Jehoiachin's captivity, the city had fallen (587 B.C.).

Following Ussher's calculations, we get 1014 B.C. for the beginning of Solomon's reign. His fourth year would be 1011 B.C., 440 years after the Exodus. That would bring the Exodus back to 1450 B.C., forty–five years earlier than calculated previously.

Here is a bird's eye view of the divided kingdom, as we interpret the data. Because the Hebrew year starts in Nisan, in spring, and because a reign may be counted from the ascension of the throne (or from the start of the next year), and because father and son sometimes ruled together, the years as given do not necessarily simply add up. (For Nisan, see Jeremiah 36:22). The total time to the fall of Jerusalem, however, is reckoned as 390 years. It may seem that we get mixed messages. See, for instance, the data for Ahaziah of Judah. We only check the bookkeeping.

Israel

Jeroboam	975–954	22 years	I Kings 14:20
Nadab	954–953	2 years	I Kings 15:25 (2nd year of Asa)
Baasha	953–930	24 years	I Kings 15:28, 33 (3rd year of Asa)
Elah	930–929	2 years	I Kings 16:8 (26th year of Asa)
Zimri	929	7 days	I Kings 16:10, 15

(Period without king till 925, I Kings 16:21–22.)

Omri	925–914	12 years	I Kings 16:23 (31st year of Asa)
Ahab	918–897	22 years	I Kings 16:29 (38th year of Asa)
Ahaziah	897–896	2 years	I Kings 22:51 (17th year of Jehoshaphat, 898)

Jehoram of Israel (Joram)	896–885	12 years	2 Kings 1:17 (2nd year of Jehoram, son of Jehoshaphat. And also 2 Kings 3:1, 18th year of Jehoshaphat king of Judah)

Judah

Rehoboam	975–959	17 years	1 Kings 14:21
Abijah	958–956	3 years	1 Kings 15:2 (18th year of Jeroboam)
Asa	955–915	41 years	1 Kings 15:9–10 (20th year of Jeroboam)
Jehoshaphat	914–890	25 years	1 Kings 22:41 (4th year of Ahab. 897, Co-reign with Jehoram)
Jehoram	891–884	8 years	2 Kings 8:16–17 (5th year of Jehoram of Israel)
Ahaziah	884	1 year	2 Kings 8:25–26 (12th year of Joram)

Notice from the two entries about Jehoram (Joram) that Jehoram son of Jehoshaphat reigned with his father nine years. This is also evident in 2 Kings 8:16–17. If Joram became king in Jehoram's second year and Jehoram reigned by himself in Joram's fifth year, we can conclude that Jehoram reigned with his father seven years.

Israel

Jehu	884–857	28 years	2 King 10:36
Jehoahaz	856–840	17 years	2 Kings 13:1 (23rd year of Joash of Judah)
Jehoash of Israel	840–825	16 years	2 Kings 13:10 (37th year of Joash of Judah, 842)
Jeroboam II	825–785	41 years	2 Kings 14:23 (15th year of Amaziah. Reigned with father 11 years before this.)
Zechariah	785–773	12 years	2 Kings 14:29
Zechariah	773	6 months	2 Kings 15:8 (38th year of Azariah)
Shallum	772	1 month	2 Kings 15:13 (39th year of Azariah)
Menahem	772–763	10 years	2 Kings 15:17 (39th year of Azariah)
Pekahiah	761–760	2 years	2 Kings 15:23 (50th year of Azariah)
Pekah	759–740	20 years	2 Kings 15:27 (52nd year of Azariah)
Hoshea	739–732	7 years	2 Kings 15:30 (20th year of Jotham)

Jotham reigned 16 years, but Ahaz is ignored because he did evil [2 Kings 16]. Hoshea is dethroned and reinstated, Compendium of World History.[110] Ahab II was king in the meantime.

Hoshea	729–721	9 years	2 Kings 17:1 (12th year of Ahaz)

---

110 Hoeh, Herman. "Compendium of World History" (1962, Volume 1). Accessed: 6 November 2010 (http://cgca.net/coglinks/wcglit/hoeh-compendium/hhc1toc.htm), p. 3.

Judah

Athaliah	884–878	6 years	Kings 11:3–4
Jehoash of Judah	878–839	40 years	2 Kings 12:1 (7th year of Jehu)
Amaziah	838–810	29 years	2 Kings 14:1–2 (2nd year of Joash of Israel)
Azariah (Uzziah)	810–759	52 years	2 Kings 15:1–2 (27th year of Jeroboam II)
Jotham	758–743	16 years	2 Kings 15:32–33 (2nd year of Pekah)
Ahaz	742–727	16 years	2 Kings 16:1–2 (17th year of Pekah)
Hezekiah	726–697	29 years	2 Kings 17:1 (12th year of Ahaz)

(In 721 B.C., 6th year of Hezekiah, Samaria carried off.)

Manasseh	697–643	55 years	2 Kings 21:1
Amon	642–641	2 years	2 Kings 21:19
Josiah	640–610	31 years	2 Kings 22:1
Jehoahaz	609	3 months	2 Kings 23:31
Jehoiakim	609–599	11 years	2 Kings 23:36 (Exiled in his 5th year)
Jehoiachin	598	3 months	2 Kings 24:8

(8th year of Nebuchadnezzar.)

Zedekiah	597–587	11 years	2 King 24:18

Israel carried off at the turn of the year 586 B.C.

Jerusalem destroyed.

This confirms the beginning of Solomon's reign.

Chapter Eight

DANIEL'S SEVENTY WEEKS

Here we answer the question of whether or not the seventy weeks provide us with a date for the birth and crucifixion of Jesus.

The First Year of Cyrus

"In the third year of the reign of Jehoiakim king of Judah came Nebuchadnezzar king of Babylon unto Jerusalem, and besieged it" (Daniel 1:1). Daniel and some other lads became exiles in Babylon. We reckon the captivity to have taken place in 605 B.C. (see previous chapter), and we use that as our reference date, not the year Jerusalem was destroyed. The exile lasted seventy years, until 536 B.C., as prophesied by Jeremiah (Jeremiah 25:11–12).

"In the first year of Darius the son of Ahasuerus, of the seed of the Medes, which was made king over the realm of the Chaldeans... I Daniel understood by books the number of the years, whereof the word of the Lord came to Jeremiah the prophet, that he would accomplish seventy years in the desolations of

Jerusalem" (Daniel 9:1–2). Close to the end of the seventy years, Daniel understands that a change in the situation draws near.

We find the reason for the captivity in Jeremiah 9:15—God will feed his people *"with wormwood, and give them water of gall to drink."* In Leviticus 26 and 28, God promised that he would punish Israel seven times for not keeping the law. *"I will scatter you among the heathen… your land shall be desolate, and your cities waste. Then shall the land enjoy her sabbaths, as long as it lieth desolate, and ye be in your enemies' land; even then shall the land rest, and enjoy her sabbaths"* (Leviticus 26:33–34).

"And Daniel continued even unto the first year of king Cyrus" (Daniel 1:21). Right away, Scripture draws our attention to that year. Daniel did not die that year. Daniel 10:1 reads, *"In the third year of Cyrus…"* That first year meant something significant. As Ezra expressed it, *"Now in the first year of Cyrus king of Persia, that the word of the Lord by the mouth of Jeremiah might be fulfilled, the Lord stirred up the spirit of Cyrus king of Persia, that he made a proclamation throughout all his kingdom, and put it also in writing, saying, Thus saith Cyrus king of Persia, The Lord God of heaven hath given me all the kingdoms of the earth; and he hath charged me to build him an house at Jerusalem, which is in Judah"* (Ezra 1:1–2).

Daniel's Prayer and the Prophecy

In Daniel 9, because he understood, Daniel confessed the sin of his nation. Daniel prayed, and from the prayer it becomes plain that God had warned Israel patiently and that in the end God had to confirm his word. Note how Daniel prayed for *"thy city Jerusalem, thy holy mountain...thy people... [and] thy sanctuary..."* (Daniel 9:16–17). God responded and Daniel receives the message about the seventy sevens. God tells him gently, "You are but praying for your city and your people." Daniel could have understood this in Daniel 7 when he learned that the saints would receive the kingdom. He then got greatly upset. Were the saints not just Israelites? In any case, the city he had prayed for was to be restored, but also it was doomed for destruction. God had bigger plans than Daniel; his plans concerned the whole world. *"My thoughts are not your thoughts"* (Isaiah 55:8). *"[God] is able to do exceeding abundantly above all that we may ask or think"* (Ephesians 3:20). Praise his name! The Messiah would be the Saviour for all people (Luke 2:10). God had promised Abraham that all nations would be blessed through him (Genesis 12:3).

Daniel 9:24 stands out: *"Seventy weeks are determined upon thy people and upon thy holy city, to finish the transgression, and to make an end of sins, and to make reconciliation for iniquity, and to bring in everlasting righteousness, and to seal up the vision and prophecy, and to anoint the most Holy."* What a promise! Can we even understand it? However, it centres on Christ.

From the commandment to restore and build Jerusalem to the coming of the Messiah, the Prince, there would be seventy weeks. These seventy weeks are divided into seven weeks, sixty–two weeks, and one week. They resemble the *"time, times and a half"* in Revelation and in Daniel. How long is that, and how should we divide the parts?

Even as the promise of salvation extends to all nations, so does the promise of God's wrath (Jeremiah 9:25–26, 25:15–33). There is none righteous, none good, for we have all fallen short of the glory of God (Romans 3:23). Understanding God's wrath makes us understand his grace in Christ. Jesus was offered vinegar and gall to drink, and he tasted of it. He took the rap for everyone, that they should be a nation dwelling safely (John 11:50–51, Matthew 21:41, 43). Instead of scattering them, God brings them home from the ends of the earth to a city whose founder and builder is God (Hebrews 11:10, Revelation 21:10) to give the true Sabbath, the true rest. Praise the Lord! That promise of salvation is given to all who acknowledge their sin, repent, and put their trust in Christ, the Messiah (John 3:16). They are the true worshippers (John 4:20–24), the true Israel (Romans 2:29), where God dwells, the temple of God (2 Corinthians 6:16). That temple surpasses anything man can make (Haggai 2:3, 7, 9).

The stone in Daniel 2 implies the same worldwide impact. Jesus remarks to the Jews about the stone, *"On whomsoever it shall fall, it will grind him to powder"* (Matthew 21:44). In Matthew 22:7, Jesus predicts the fall of Jerusalem a second time. Similar cities or nations may expect the same—say, New York or New Orleans. God is no respecter of cities or nations (Daniel 4:35). This destruction awaits all nations that build without God, the Creator of heaven and earth! Unless the Lord build the house, its builders build in vain; unless the Lord keep the city, the watchers watch in vain (Psalms 127:1); no homeland security will protect them.

Except the Lord build the house, they labour in vain. (Psalms 127:1)

I am the Lord… there is no God beside me. (Isaiah 45:5)

And great was the fall of it. (Matthew 7:27)

Christ saves unto the uttermost everyone who puts his trust in him. That includes the Jews and the Moslems and all others. By the testimony of two or three, it shall stand. God is three in one. He cannot lie. In him we see perfect authority, perfect obedience, and perfect love. He keeps his word. This earth is destined for destruction (2 Peter 3:10–11), but salvation has come through the anointed Jesus, his grace and truth. For Christ we wait, and say, *"Even so, come, Lord Jesus"* (Revelation 22:20). In the prophecy, Jesus is the subject; can it be otherwise?

THE TIME OF THE PROPHECY

The prophecy starts with a decree to build Jerusalem. When was that decree? Only one answer can be given: when Cyrus spoke and wrote. Cyrus said that the Lord had charged him. The seventy–year captivity that Jeremiah had prophesied had ended. The Jews returned to build Jerusalem. The temple and the city with the walls belonged together. A city without walls was unthinkable. Cyrus and all the Jews understood it that way. According to Isaiah 44:28, Cyrus spoke to Jerusalem, *"[Cyrus] is my shepherd, and shall perform all my pleasure...Thou shalt be built; and to the temple, Thy foundations shall be laid."* Cyrus means *Kurios,* or "Lord." He typified Jesus, who will build the real temple of God, the temple made without hands. *All* the promises of God are bound up in Jesus, not just some of them. This counts as the start of the seventy sevens, and they end with Jesus. God does not speak of years and, though men usually assume it, we cannot work it out to **490 years**.

Also because of the prophecies in Isaiah, the Jews understood that they could build the city and the walls, and they understood rightly.[111] By various contortions, men have

---

111   Josephus, *Antiquities of the Jews*, Eighth Edition (Grand Rapids, MI: Kregal Publications, 1970), Book XI, p. 228. Copyright held by William Whiston. Cyrus promised that "he would be their assistant, and write to the governors in the neighbourhood of their country of Judea, that they

tried to fit historical facts to their assumptions. History does not conform.

Because the city, the nation, the temple, and the walls are bound together into one, the prophecy does not require a special decree to build the walls of Jerusalem. That is a lie of the devil. It is only accepted to fit the prophecy to an interpretation of 490 years, but it ignores scripture. When the literalists and legalists came and said that they had no permission, the Jews swallowed the lie. Should we still swallow it? Does only the decree to Nehemiah (Nehemiah 2:8) fulfill the decree to build the walls? That requirement is a red herring, and that decree was not issued by Longimanus, but by Hystaspes.

The promised events happened, but not at the end of 487 years. Neither can we tell where the first seven weeks ended. We would think that they ended at the completion of the temple, or at the completion of the walls of Jerusalem, but they do not. Just as we cannot tell when the *"time, times and a half"* in Revelation begin or end in a fixed timeframe, we cannot pinpoint a time of 487 years here, and we cannot insist on them.

The chronology from Daniel to Christ does not fit our expectations, but God does not lie or cater to our beloved preconceptions. God is sovereign, and his ways are beyond

---

should contribute to them gold and silver for the building of the temple, and, besides that, beasts for their sacrifices." Josephus quotes letters to Sisinnes and Sathrabuzanes. Our Bible calls them Tatnai and Shetharboznai (Ezra 5:15_. In Scripture they knew nothing about these letters, or pretended not to know.

our ability to discover (Romans 11:33). It was no different then from now: *"Blessed are they who wait for their Lord"* (Luke 12:37, 2 Timothy 4:8). Calculation cannot save us. Only faith will please God, not the wisdom of the princes of this world. If the princes had known, they would not have crucified the Lord of glory (1 Corinthians 2:6–8).

In the midst of the last week, he will cause the sacrifice and the oblation to cease (Daniel 9:27). The emphasis falls on the crucifixion in the middle of the last week, and also on a Wednesday. Jesus was in the grave three days and three nights—Thursday, Friday, and Saturday. Lazarus was in the grave on the fourth day when Martha said of him, "He stinks." Jesus then tarried in the grave no less than three days. Jesus told Martha, *"Did I not say to you that if you believe you will see the glory of God?"* (John 11:40, NKJV) When Jesus himself arose, truly they beheld his glory (John 1:14). Jesus is the resurrection and the life. He is Mahalalel Jared, the glory of God come down. He conquered death. Christ himself was the accepted sacrifice. The sacrifices in the temple became only so much ritual. God is true. It's a new day.

Who is Artaxerxes?

Here we concern ourselves with identifying the Artaxerxes of Ezra and of Nehemiah. Many mistake Artaxerxes Longimanus for Artaxerxes of Ezra and of Nehemiah. In some bibles, the books of Ezra and Nehemiah are introduced with the statement that Ezra and Nehemiah came to Jerusalem about a hundred years after the Jews returned. The Scofield Bible and the New International Version tell you this, but it's not true. Ultimately, Christ is Artaxerxes, Ahasuerus, King of kings. He is Lord. He builds the New Temple that will last forever.

These are kings of Persia from Darius the Mede onward.[112]

- Darius the Mede, 538–537, 2 years.

- Cyrus the Great (Ahasuerus), 536–528, 9 years.

- Cambyses (Artaxerxes), 528–521, 8 years.

- Darius Hystaspes (Ahasuerus, KJV; Artaxerxes, LXX), 521–484, 36 years.

- Xerxes, 483–463, 21 years. Father received annual tribute, and therefore was rich (Daniel 11:2).

- Artaxerxes Longimanus, 464–424, 41 years.

Nehemiah 5:14 says that Neheniah was governor in Jerusalem from the twentieth to the thirty–second year of Artaxerxes. From the table, we note that only two kings ruled longer than 32 years—Hystaspes and Longimanus. The problem with Hystaspes is that he does not fit the 490–year timeframe. Some eclipses and other astronomical data confirm that his reign started in 521 B.C.,[113] whereas if you go back 490 or 483 years from the cross (A.D. 30 or 31), you come to Longimanus, or 453 B.C., to be

---

[112] Source unknown. A similar table is found in *The Chronology of the Old Testament*, by Dr. Floyd Nolen Jones, p. 201.

[113] Newton, Isaac. "The Chronology of Ancient Kingdoms Amended," Chapter VI. Accessed: 6 November 2010 (http://www.gutenberg.org/files/15784/15784–h/15784–h.html#chapVI).

more exact. Only, his twentieth year when he supposedly allowed the building of the wall, should be 445 B.C. Someone once claimed that Artaxerxes (Longimanus) reigned together with his father. However, Carl Olof Jonsson has clearly proved that we simply cannot doctor the case to appear that way.[114]

Although we might accept all that, because 487 years back bring us to Longimanus, somehow he and his decree should still be the start of the seventy sevens. We still need to identify Artaxerxes.

EZRA. ARTAXERXES IS DARIUS, NOT LONGIMANUS.

In his first year, in 536 B.C., Cyrus proclaims liberty for the Jews to go back to Jerusalem and build the temple. The Jews were under the leadership of Shesbazzar, which was probably his Persian name, though he was also known as Zerubbabel. Ezra the scribe provides a list of the people of the province who came with Zerubbabel, and this list deserves special attention. In Ezra 3, we read that they kept the feast of Tabernacles in the seventh month, and after that they kept all the feasts of the Lord. Ezra makes no mention of his own role at the time, but in Nehemiah 8 we find out that he read the Law of Moses. In the second month of the second year, they celebrated the laying of the foundation of the temple. Many shouted for joy, but many of those who had seen the first house wept aloud. In 586

---

114 Jonsson, Carl Olof. "The 20th year of Artaxerxes and the 'Seventy Weeks' of Daniel." Accessed: 6 November 2010 (http://user.trinet.se/~00f408u/fhf/english/artaxerxes.htm).

B.C. the temple met its end. Fifty years later, many who had seen the previous temple still remembered it.

Several kinds of people lived in Israel then (Ezra 4:2, 10). They troubled the Jews during the time of Cyrus until the reign of Darius (Ezra 4:5). They wrote to "Ahasuerus" in the beginning of his reign, and again to "Artaxerxes." On their instigation, he (Cambyses) made the Jews cease. The devil is a legalist and the Jews could not refute the arguments of their adversaries until the second year of Darius (Ezra 4:24). The work lay still for nine years.[115] They even stopped building the temple which Cyrus had commanded. In that second year, encouraged by the prophets Haggai (Ezra 1:1 and Zechariah 1:1), the Jews decided to start building again. Zerubbabel claimed authority by Cyrus and appealed to Darius. The Jews kept on building and Cyrus' letter was found. In his second year, Darius decreed that the temple be finished, sixteen years after the Jews first returned.

In the decree we read, *"That they may offer sacrifices of sweet savours unto the God of heaven, and pray for the life of the king, and of his sons"* (Ezra 6:10). Now the Jews claimed authority by God, Cyrus, Darius, and "Artaxerxes." In Ezra 6:14, Artaxerxes is mentioned again, but this is certainly not the one who reigned before Darius Hystaspes, and certainly not Longimanus. A great deal of time passed between the order to stop building and the order to start building again. Different kings issued those orders. Nobody changed his

---

[115] Josephus, *Antiquities of the Jews*, Eighth Edition (Grand Rapids, MI: Kregal Publications, 1970), Book XI, p. 2. Copyright held by William Whiston.

mind, although Artaxerxes, who stopped the construction, reserved in his letter the right to change his mind (Ezra 4:21), to circumvent the law of the Medes and Persians, which could not be changed.

We should take Ezra 6:14 very much like Mark 16:7, saying "Tell the disciples and Peter." Peter *was* a disciple. Those words were meant for Peter in particular. Here was meant Darius, the one called Artaxerxes, the king of Persia, or also called Darius the Persian, because there was a previous Darius, the Mede. Ahasuerus and Artaxerxes are actually titles, not names, and therefore the implied question—"Which Darius do you mean?"—was answered. In Ezra 6:15, the reference to Artaxerxes refers to Darius Hystaspes.

The house of the Lord was finished on the third of Adar, the twelfth month of the sixth year of Darius (516 B.C.), known as Darius the Great, Artaxerxes and Ahasuerus (Ezra 6:15). Longimanus was still to come. The dedication and Passover took place in the next month, the first month of the year. It was a time of rejoicing—*"for the Lord had made them joyful, and turned the heart of the king of Assyria unto them, to strengthen their hands in the work of the house of God, the God of Israel"* (Ezra 6:22).

In Ezra 7, Ezra finally talks about himself. On the first of Nisan, within thirty days of completion of the temple, Ezra left for Jerusalem (Ezra 7:7), arriving on the first of the fifth month of the seventh year of Artaxerxes, 515 B.C. (Ezra 7:9). This was also about the time that the king commissioned the inscription on the rock of Behistan, proclaiming his achievements. In the book of Esther, we are told that in his third year Ahasuerus (King Artaxerxes, Darius) ruled 127 provinces. God had made him to prosper and he assumed more titles. God had kept his promise to Abraham: *"I will bless them that bless thee"* (Genesis 12:3). The king recognized his blessings and was quite ready to further support work on the temple. The investment made sense. To even speak of Longimanus now, since we have already met with the title of Artaxerxes several times, is not reasonable. It is too much of a leap. Our table shows that between Darius and Longimanus we have a span of 57 years.

Ezra was the son of Seraiah. Both came from exile with Zerubbabel (Ezra 2:2, Nehemiah 12:1). When Ezra returned to Jerusalem again, he brought Levites with him to serve in the newly finished temple and treasure for furnishings and sacrifices (Ezra 7:6, 8:15–17). He had apparently gone back to Babylon, probably after the work was stopped. Note that this is only twenty-two years after Israel first returned.

Obviously, if Ezra were present in the beginning, at least in his twenties, he would not arrive in Jerusalem a hundred years later. He would then be over a hundred and twenty years old.

NEHEMIAH. ARTAXERXES IS NOT LONGIMANUS.

Thirteen years after Ezra, we find Nehemiah in Shushan in the month of Chisleu of the twentieth year of Artaxerxes (Nehemiah 2:1). Hanani, a brother of Nehemiah, and some others came to talk about Jerusalem. Things did not go well. The strangers opposed and harassed the Jews constantly, and the fact that the walls still lay in ruins did not help. These visitors brought Nehemiah up to date and they hoped he could put in a good word for Jerusalem with the king; Nehemiah was the king's cupbearer, and the king had shown kindness to the Jews before.

Also, Nehemiah had originally come to Jerusalem along with Zerubbabel (Ezra 2:2 and Nehemiah 10:1). He was apparently co–regent, Tirshata (Ezra 2:63). The returnees had come hoping to build the temple, but many had left and became otherwise engaged once the project came to a halt. Nehemiah felt depressed with the news, and may have wondered how to approach the king about it. In the month of Nisan, still the twentieth year of Artaxerxes, he spoke with the king and obtained authority to rebuild the walls (Nehemiah 2:6). The king stood behind his previous decrees. Nehemiah mentions that the queen sat beside the king. She was Esther. Less than seven years earlier, Esther had revealed to the king that she was Jewish.

Obviously, if Nehemiah returned in the first year of Cyrus, at least in his twenties, he would not arrive in Jerusalem a hundred years later. He would also be over a hundred and twenty years old.

In Nehemiah 3, Eliashib the high priest rose to build the wall. Since this is now thirty–five years after the Jews first returned with Zerubbabel, let us see who is still around and meet their sons.

- Binnui son of Henadad, was a Levite. We met him when he signed the sealed document.
- The high priest, Eliashib, is a grandson of Jeshua. He came with Zerubbabel. Shortly after Ezra's arrival, Ezra mentions Jehohanan the son of Eliashib (Ezra 10:6).
- Pahath–Moab was a leader who sealed the document. His son Hasshub and granddaughters worked on the wall.
- Malchijah son of Harim worked together with Hasshub. He sealed, repented, and built (Nehemiah 3:11).
- Meremoth, a priest and son of Uriah, arrived with Zerubbabel (Nehemiah 12:1, 3) and at that time sealed the covenant along with Nehemiah (Nehemiah 10:5). He received the treasure from Ezra (Ezra 8:33), and also repented (Ezra 10:36). He worked on the wall (Nehemiah 3:4, 21). If he built the wall in the time of Longimanus, he would have been very old indeed. He was at least 56 years old.
- Rehum the son of Bani, who stood on Ezra's left when he read, looked after the Levites working on the wall.
- Parosh sealed the document, and may have been the grandfather of Shemaiah, the son of Col–Hozeh.

In the time of Longimanus, these men or their sons would not have been around, only their grandsons and great-grandsons.

The people worked on the wall and kept the sword handy. They kept their clothes on except for when they washed them. The walls were indeed built in troubled times (Daniel 9:25), but they finished the wall on the twenty-fifth day of Elul, in fifty-two days. Nehemiah then put his brother Hanani and someone else in charge of Jerusalem (Nehemiah 7:2).

Nehemiah was *tirshata*, a supervisory governor, for twelve years, from the twentieth to the thirty-second year of Artaxerxes (Nehemiah 5:14, 13:6). Only Hystaspes qualifies for this Artaxerxes; Longimanus came on the scene too late. At the end of the twelve years, Nehemiah was at least sixty-six years old. Let's not add fifty-seven years. Apparently Eliashib was still high priest.

When the Israelites first returned from exile, they sealed a covenant to do better than their forefathers. Ezra reported corruption when he returned (Ezra 9), and Nehemiah reported corruption in high places before his time, and again at the end of the twelve years (Nehemiah 9, 13). Whither Israel? They also need a Saviour.

Esther

We read in Daniel 6 that Darius, son of Ahasuerus, of the seed of the Medes, set one hundred and twenty princes over the kingdom. Cyrus, after he conquered Babylon, went on to further conquests. That's why Esther explains, *"This is Ahasuerus which reigned, from India even unto Ethiopia, over an hundred and seven and twenty provinces"* (Esther 1:1). Since Ahasuerus was not a personal name but a title, we therefore have the distinguishing descriptions. The Septuagint calls him Artaxerxes.

King Ahasuerus held a feast in his third year (Esther 1:3). Esther entered the palace as queen in the tenth month of the seventh year of Ahasuerus (Esther 2:16). (This is the year Ezra went to Jerusalem.) In the twelfth year of Ahasuerus, the king and his advisors cast lots to decide about the Jews from month to month until the month of Adar; Haman hated the Jews. The next year, Haman expected to destroy the Jews, but the fourteenth day of Adar became a day of celebration for the Jews.

In Daniel 8, Daniel has a vision in which he is in Shushan in a palace or fort. He saw this in the third year of the reign of Belshazzar, before the Persians conquered Babylon. He saw Persia as a ram pushing westward, northward, and southward until it met a one-horned he-goat. The ram was moving for Greece and the Mediterranean islands, Egypt, and Ethiopia. It had two high horns, but one was bigger than the other and the higher one came up later. When Babylon was conquered Darius was a Mede, Cyrus a Persian. We read of the law of Medes and Persians, not of Persians and Medes. Later on, the Persians became more dominant. One horn had become bigger. When Persia clashed with Greece, the ram and the he-goat of the vision met.

In Daniel 11, in the first year of Cyrus, Gabriel tells Daniel that in the first year of Darius (the Mede) he fought *with*, not against, the prince of Persia and supported him. Darius the Mede reigned only two years. *"Behold, there shall stand up yet three kings in Persia; and the fourth shall be far richer than they all: and by his strength through his riches he shall stir up all against the realm of Grecia."* (Daniel 11:2). Gabriel said, *"When I am gone forth, lo, the prince of Grecia shall come"* (Daniel 10:20). Here is a second witness to Greece taking over (Genesis 41:32). It is established; it will happen soon.

That fourth king we understand to be Xerxes. He spent all his wealth to subdue Greece. Although Longimanus reigned for forty-one years, from this prophecy we take it that, in essence, the power of Persia had been broken. Under Darius the Great, Persia reached the height of its power.

Dr. Floyd Nolen Jones explains why Ahasuerus of Esther had a council of seven.[116] Those before him did not have such a council. Floyd Jones also points out that Darius Hystaspes raised taxes after his twelfth year of reign, but Xerxes had already lost the islands before his twelfth year.[117] Cambyses had conquests in Ethiopia but did not receive an annual tribute. Ahasuerus (Darius Hystaspes) did (Esther 10:1). He is the only ruler who reigned long enough to be the Artaxerxes of Ezra and Nehemiah. The Septuagint calls Ahasuerus of the book of Esther Artaxerxes. Again the LXX at times has things straighter than the Masoretic.

---

116 Jones, Floyd Nolen. *The Chronology of the Old Testament*, 15th Edition (Green Forest, AR: Masterbooks, 2005), p. 200.
117 Ibid., pp. 200–203.

Conclusion

The references in the book of Esther to historical events, and more pertinently to secular documents (Esther 10:2)—such as the chronicles of Persia—indicate that God places no premium on ignorance. Paul also asks that books be brought back to him (2 Timothy 4:13). Moses was learned in all the wisdom of the Egyptians, and Daniel in Babylonian learning. The Jews adopted Babylonian names for the months of the year. God desires truth in the inward parts; his Word takes first place. God is in the midst of history. He is its author, and his Word does not stand apart from life.

This is not just history; it is prophecy. Cyrus portrays the Lord, the Christ. He *"shall perform all my pleasure"* (Isaiah 44:28). Amen. The temple, the city, and the wall were all of one piece. God in Christ gives us a temple, a city, a safe country, and protection—all in one. They are forever. No enemy shall ever threaten them; peace will reign. God's walls are salvation. Hallelujah!

Note: As mentioned, the expression *"time, times and a half,"* or something similar, is found in Daniel at least three times. In Daniel 7, we get the explanation of the term. We should see it as a contrast to the kingdom in Daniel 7:14 and 7:27, the kingdom that will not be destroyed. The kingdoms portrayed by the beasts last only a short time. Their dominion was taken away, and they were given an extension of life for an appointed season and time (Daniel 7:12). Their terror may seem endless, but only a set time is allotted to them. The Lord will make of them a short end.

This is the scriptural interpretation. At least four of the Old Testament books witness to none but Cyrus—Isaiah, Jeremiah, Daniel, and Ezra. To think instead of any other person, say Darius or Artaxerxes, is unscriptural. Let it be anathema. Salvation begins with the Lord, the Word, the Alpha and Omega, the beginning and the end. Only Cyrus pictures the Lord.

Darius Hystaspes approved the building of the temple. He sent Ezra to furnish the temple, and married Esther, appointed Mordecai, and approved the walls of Jerusalem. On this rock near Behistan his victories are recorded.

Chapter Nine

ON REVELATION

Having referred to the end of the world in the first chapter, I here want to expand on that. Revelation is probably the most misunderstood book in the Bible, and therefore gives rise to a lot of myths. The Bible tells the truth about the past, and also about the future. John is shown in symbols things that must occur hereafter, but Revelation speaks foremost about Jesus, and it begins and ends with him. All scripture is profitable (2 Timothy 3:16) in order to explain the symbols (2 Peter 1:20). We will compare spiritual things, but dark texts will not explain plain ones (1 Corinthians 2:11–16). In Revelation, we do not have a crystal ball; soothsaying is an abomination. God's angel signified to John; he talked to John in symbols. The Old Testament has been called the Law, and that is also true of the New Testament. We will look for precedents, second witnesses.

John hears of *"things which must shortly come to pass"* (Revelation 1:1). In Genesis, we saw that pharaoh's two dreams meant the same thing: *"For that the dream was doubled unto Pharaoh twice; it is because the thing is established by God, and God will shortly bring it to pass"* (Genesis 41:32). So these things also must happen right away, not just before Christ returns. This we read seven times (Revelation 1:1, 3, Revelation 22:6, 7, 10, 12, and 20).

Scripture's frequent use of the number seven refers to totality, fullness, perfection, or divinity, just as seven days comprise a full week. Abraham and Mary are encouraged seven times. God's wisdom rests on seven pillars (Proverbs 9:1), not just five. Revelation 5:12 ascribes seven things to Jesus. In Revelation, John falls down before the angel twice, and twice the angel told him not to do that, but to worship God (Revelation 19:10 and 22:8). Indeed, in three gospels Jesus receives worship seven times without a word of protest. Jesus is God, I AM. Jesus is the Amen of God (Revelation 3:14). He that believes on him has set to a seal that God is true. Joseph's years of plenty were perfect, and there was a perfect drought. Clearly, with the seven churches God addresses the whole Church, then and now. Have an ear.

The seven repetitions of Revelation present different aspects of the same timespan, but each glorifies Christ. He is worthy! He was born the king of the Jews. His kingdom is reckoned from when Jesus started his ministry until the time he returns. He started his ministry with the saying, *"Repent: for the kingdom of heaven is at hand"* (Matthew 4:17). Jesus preached and demonstrated the good news of the kingdom (Matthew 4:17, 23, Mark 1:14, 15, 27). On his cross Pilate ordered a sign which read, "Jesus the Nazarene, King of the Jews." After the resurrection Jesus told the apostles, *"All power is given unto me...Go ye therefore, and teach all nations, baptizing them in the name of the Father, and of the Son, and of the Holy Ghost"* (Matthew 28:18–19). *"Go ye into all the world, and preach the gospel..."* (Mark 16:15). And they preached, God confirming the word with signs and wonders (Mark 16:20). He still does. He is our King, and of the increase of his government there shall be no end (Isaiah 9:6, Luke 1:33).

The time of the kingdom has been designated variously seven times, meaning that God allots the earth all this time, no more. These texts are Revelation 11:2, 11:3, 12:6, 12:14, 13:5, 20:2, and 20:6. They each differ but point to the same thing. The siege of a city was usually given in months, and therefore "Jerusalem" is besieged 42 months. What God's people do, they do every day (Proverbs 11:27), and therefore it talks about 1,260 days. *"A time, times and a half"* means a certain time and a long time, but it ends with a short period of time for the sake of God's people (Proverbs 13:12, Matthew 24:22, Mark 13:20). The 1,000 years also refer to a certain time, a long time, and again they end with a short time. The souls under the altar cry out, "How long, oh Lord?" The answer is that they must rest yet for a little season (Revelation 6:10–11). This reminds me of Luke 18:8, where it says, *"I tell you that he will avenge them speedily."* So, the 1,000 years take place right now. The days, months, and years are all numbered; they are limited. There comes an end.

In Genesis 49, the Bible first speaks of the last days. Jacob tells his sons what will then happen to them. Of Judah, he says that when Shilo (he that is worthy) comes, the sceptre and the lawgiver will depart from him. Does God add anything to that? Shall we? Shilo came. In the year A.D. 70, Israel was no longer a nation. In Revelation 5:2–5, who is worthy but Jesus? Daniel 2:28 and on speaks of this kingdom as existing in *"the latter days."* God tells Daniel to seal the book until *"the time of the end"* (Daniel 12:4), whereas he commands John not to seal the book, because the time is at hand (Revelation 22:10). In Acts, Peter quotes the prophet Joel that in the last days God will pour out his Spirit (Acts 2:17). Paul and James also agree with this (2 Timothy 3:1, James 5:3). John even speaks of the last hour (1 John 2:18). We live in the last days. Should we then expect another dispensation?

In John 5:21–26, Jesus speaks of the new birth as a resurrection. *"He that heareth my word, and believeth on him that sent me, hath everlasting life, and shall not come into condemnation; but is passed from death unto life"* (John 5:24). Ezekiel 37, with its description of the valley of dead bones, spoke of the same. There is only one resurrection to come, of both the just and the unjust (John 5:28). All those that are in the grave will hear his voice. See also Acts 24:15. Jesus had taught about the last day (John 6:39–54). In John 11:24, Martha said that Lazarus would rise again at the last day. Since unbelievers will not rise again until the end of the 1,000 years (Revelation 20:5–6), Lazarus must belong with them, if the 1,000 years were yet another dispensation still coming. It's not so. That they will be judged in the same last day is clear from John 12:48—"*He that rejecteth me, and receiveth not my words, hath one that judgeth him: the word that I have spoken, the same shall judge him in the last day."* There is only one last day. We live in the last days, and they began 2,000 years ago (James 5:3, 5:8–9, and 1 Peter 4:5). Blessed is he who takes part in the first resurrection. The second death has no power over him. Do you know that resurrection? Jesus is the resurrection, and he raised Lazarus. God is not the God of the dead but of the living (John 8:51, 11:26, Matthew 22:32).

We live in perilous times (2 Timothy 3:1) and in Scripture we are encouraged seven times. It may seem that Satan rules. Christ's blood avails for all our sins. He is in the midst of the candlesticks. He holds us in his hands. We are seated with him in heavenly places (Ephesians 2:9–11). We reign in life by him (Romans 5:17, Revelation 2:26–27, 5:10, 20:6). Christ has made us kings and priests (Revelation 1:6), more than conquerors (Romans 8:37). Even as Christ overcame and is seated on the throne with his Father, so will Christ grant him, who overcomes, to sit on the throne with himself (Revelation 3:21). In Revelation 5:10, note the expression *"on the earth,"* and in Revelation 20:6 note *"reign with him a thousand years."* Is the work of the priest not just for this world? Just as Adam was meant to reign, so also are we to reign with Christ. We are free from the curse. Now are the thousand years.

Until Christ came, the people were in darkness (Matthew 4:16). Soon the gospel spread to all the Gentiles. Romans

1:8 and Matthew 24:14 tell us that this gospel of the kingdom will be preached in the whole world for a witness to all nations, and then shall the end come. Satan was bound a thousand years (Revelation 20:2–3). Christ took his captives (Matthew 12:29, Luke 4:18). Satan at the end will surround the camp of the saints for a short while (Revelation 20:9). God is sovereign, but not arbitrary. There is a reason for all this and Matthew 12:43–45 gives it. Once an evil spirit is driven out and comes back with his friends, things will be worse. Even so shall it be to this wicked generation. Christ had come and his own received him not. We have no king but Caesar, a foreigner (Deuteronomy 17:15). In A.D. 70, Jerusalem was destroyed, about 74 years after Christ was born. Judgment was not long. So it will be with all nations, but for the sake of the elect those days will be shortened (Mark 13:19–20, Psalms 2:1–3, Acts 4:25–26).

Did Paul say that we live in perilous times? Times are more perilous today than ever before, and we need encouragement. When you see these things, know that the time is near. For the sake of the elect, the time will be cut short. Let not the saints be lulled to sleep, saying that things are not too bad; wait until you see the tribulation. Watch and pray. We need not fear these things, but we need to fear falling into the hands of the living God. It will be like in the days of Noah, people marrying and being given in marriage. Know, however, that more saints die today than ever before (Revelation 6:11). Maybe not in our part of the world—though for how long will this be true?—but know that if one member suffers, the whole body suffers! Are you comforted or concerned? Be both.

"The gates of hell shall not prevail against it" (Matthew 16:18) means that the Church of God, God himself, is on the move. The blood of the martyrs is the seed of the Church. This is the Church militant. *"In the world ye shall have tribulation: but be of good cheer; I have overcome the world"* (John 16:33). *"Greater is he that is in you, than he that is in the world"* (1 John 4:4). *"[Yet] the bush was not consumed,"* Moses said (Exodus 3:2). When the sheep number 144,000, when the last person is saved and enters the fold, the door will be closed.

Nicolaitan churches that are governed from the top down, like the Roman church, are upset over the inroads of the Church. Watch out for the leaven of the Pharisees among you, or your candlestick will be removed. Watch and pray. Have an ear to hear.

In 1 Corinthians 15:26, we read that death will be defeated last. We will hear the last trump (15:52), when Christ returns to judge the quick and the dead, on the last day. Until then, Christ sits and intercedes (Romans 8:34). *"Sit thou at my right hand, until I make thine enemies thy footstool"* (Psalms 110:1). Then he leaves that position and intercession ceases. When Christ returns, the saints will rise to be with him forever. The notion that there will be yet another thousand years after these *last days* is myth.

In 1 Corinthians 15:46, Paul tells us that the physical comes first, then the spiritual. It would make no sense for God to go back to a physical kingdom—physical Israel. Jesus said that his kingdom is not of this earth, and that the kingdom of God comes not with observation (Luke 17:20). Should we, like the Jews, look for a physical kingdom? Then what would be the significance of Jesus? God gave his only Son, so that whoever believes on him should not perish but have eternal life, including the Jews. Can we expect more? Jesus fulfilled the promise given in Eden, not Moses. Christ came and he shall save his people from their sins (Matthew 1:21, Luke 1:32, Jeremiah 23:5–7). In the beginning was the Word, and the Word was God. Let us not take away from his glory. There will be no other dispensation on this earth. Peter, speaking about the return of the Lord, says, *"The heavens shall pass away with a great noise, and the elements shall melt with fervent heat, the earth also and the works that are therein shall be burned up"* (2 Peter 3:10). There is not a word about a 1,000-year kingdom. This is not a cat and mouse game.

If God plays any game, I would say it is Hide and Seek, but the repetition of the sevens begs us to find him, whom to know is life eternal. *"I love them that love me; and those that seek me early [diligently] shall find me"* (Proverbs 8:17). His eyes go to and fro to see on whose behalf he may show himself strong (2 Chronicles 16:9). Ask, seek, and knock!

Everybody ought to know who Jesus is. In Ezekiel, we commonly meet the phrase, *"And they shall know that I am the Lord."* This is the purpose of Revelation. Nebuchadnezzar's exile served the same purpose (Daniel 4:3, 25). Only here it concerns the whole world, not just one person. Every knee shall bow (Ephesians 2:9–11, Revelation 4:11). Mission accomplished. The recognition of this will be after seven times have passed over men. Time shall be no more. Unbelievers will cry, "Alas, alas." God's people will rejoice.

Revelation mentions the 144,000, the full number of God's servants (Revelation 7 and 14), who are sealed with the Holy Spirit of promise (Ephesians 1:13). All believers are the seed of Abraham (Romans 9:8, Galatians 3:29). He is no Jew, who is one outwardly (Romans 2:28–29), but who is one inwardly. In Christ there is neither Jew nor Gentile (Galatians 3:28). In short, the 144,000 are all Jews inwardly. If Revelation spoke of Israel according to the flesh, Reuben would have been mentioned first, not Judah. Also, Ephraim and Dan would have been mentioned. This is not replacement theology but implant theology (Romans 11:24).

Acts 15:16, in connection to the Gentiles, says that God will again build the tent of David. These words in Acts 15 come from Amos 9:11. Ezekiel 37:24, Isaiah 11, and others are possible. Actually, here we get another reason for the destruction of Jerusalem, and the temple. Jesus called the temple "my Father's house." From the time the Holy Ghost came down, the Church is the body of Christ. God's people are now his abode, Christ in you, the hope of glory (John 14:23, 1 Peter 2:5, Hebrews 3:6, Colossians 1:27, 1 Corinthians 3:16, 2 Corinthians 6:16, Revelation 3:20). No longer do we need a physical temple. We never will.

Please note that in all this I have referred to Scripture as promised at the start. It takes faith, the substance of things hoped for, the evidence of things not seen. By it Abraham looked for a city which has a foundation, whose builder and maker is God. Without faith we cannot please God. We only need to take God at his Word. The kingdom of God is within you. By faith Paul looked not upon things that are seen, but on those that are not seen, which are eternal (2 Corinthians 4:18). It is a biblical principle to compare spiritual things with spiritual, as we read in 1 Corinthians 2:13. I have not done any allegorizing beyond that of Scripture itself. We do well to study to show ourselves approved (2 Timothy 2:15), that we indeed may worship in Spirit and in truth. We cannot suffer contradictions. We do not use our own imagination, and we do not twist Scripture (2 Peter 3:16). *"Thy Word is a lamp unto my feet"* (Psalms 119:105). Praise the Lord. Give him the glory.

Chapter Ten

THE SABBATH

We add this part for at least two reasons. Every fable and false doctrine takes away from the glory of God and comes under the heading of myth. This continues from my discussion of Revelation. Like Revelation, the Sabbath is all about Jesus. In these last days, God has spoken to us by his Son (Hebrews 1:1–2, Matthew 17:5). In the fullness of time he sent him, born under the law (Galatians 4:4). He is the way to salvation and there is no other. He fulfilled the law for us.

The Sabbath in the Old Testament

God first instituted the Sabbath after he had finished creation. God created man last, and prepared all things for his arrival, *"and behold, it was very good"* (Genesis 1:31). God rested on the seventh day and took delight in his creation, and it speaks of his love for us (Genesis 2:3). God desires fellowship with us who are made in his image; he wants us to rest and delight in him and his creation, to discriminate between things and delight in the differences between them, to consider his works and his order. Adam named all things. First you shall love the Lord your God with all that is within you, and equal to that your neighbour as yourself. God blessed the day and sanctified it. Shall God bless us if we slight him? There was no law, but observing the Sabbath was the way to worship God, to do as he does, to glory in him.

Known to God are all his works from the beginning (Acts 15:18). He chose us in Christ Jesus from before the foundation of the world. When God made separation between the waters below and above the firmament on the second day, in the Masoretic it only says that it was so; for all the other days Scripture said it was good. Those waters were the demise of the wicked in the Flood. God takes no delight in the death of the wicked.

Now, after man's fall into sin, God had another job, the work of salvation. This was the promise to the serpent in the garden: *"I will put enmity between thee and the woman, and between thy seed and her seed; it shall bruise thy head"* (Genesis 3:15). With that, he already announced the virgin birth of the Saviour.

As explained in Chapter One, the string of names of the pre–Flood patriarchs announced the gospel in a nutshell. The name "Noah" signifies "rest." Jesus is our rest. By his death he made peace for us. We do not work, but rest in him. In wrath God remembers mercy (Habakkuk 3:2).

Exodus 16:1–27 indicates that the fifteenth day of the second month after Israel left Egypt was a Sabbath. That day they set forth from Elim and complained, but at night the quail came down, now being the sixteenth day. In the morning came the manna. This manna came every day from then on, for six days a week. No manna was on the ground on the twenty-second day of the month, the seventh day. So on the twenty-second of the second month, Israel celebrated the first Sabbath. Jesus said, *"I am the bread of life"* (John 6:35).

In Exodus 20:11, God first tells us why he ordained the Sabbath: *"For in six days the Lord made the heaven and the earth, the sea, and all that in them is, and rested the seventh day; wherefore the Lord blessed the sabbath day, and hallowed it."* That harkens back to Genesis 2:2–3. This time it is a law, a work. He that does not keep the Sabbath—one who chooses to gather wood, for instance—is worthy of death (Numbers 15:35). The offence causes one to forfeit his life. Jeremiah 17 explains this penalty as being the cause of Israel's seventy-year deportation to Babylon. We have all come short of the glory of God. No man shall be justified by the works of the law. But the coming of the law did not make the promise of no effect. The law was for our good, which is why it is repeated so often. The law pointed us to the need of a Saviour.

Deuteronomy 5:15 gives us the other historical reason (not to say that Creation was not historical). *"Remember that thou wast a servant in the land of Egypt, and that the Lord thy God brought thee out thence through a mighty hand and by a stretched out arm: therefore the Lord thy God commanded thee to keep the sabbath day."* Egypt was the house of bondage, the iron furnace, and there was no rest there.

1 Corinthians identifies the rock in the desert as Jesus. Similarly, Isaiah 53:1 and Luke 1:51 identify the arm of the Lord as Jesus. *"For unto you is born this day in the city of David a Saviour, which is Christ the Lord"* (Luke 2:11). Jesus gives deliverance from sin—rest! The Sabbath therefore pointed forward to Jesus. He is our rest. By the same token (Exodus 31:15), he who does not keep this rest shall be cut off (Galatians 3:10, 5:4). The Galatians did not. Paul curses the Judaizers twice. Love fulfills the law (Galatians 5:14); this is the law of Christ (Galatians 6:2).

The First of the Week in the Old Testament

For this, we need to look at the third holy feast of Israel in the Old Testament. First off, we should remember that the Old Testament testifies to Jesus. It does so in the feast of first fruits. The Israelites first celebrated this feast when they entered the Promised Land; it was a Thanksgiving Day; our Promised Land is our life in Christ. The feast of Passover started on the fourteenth day of Nissan; the feast of unleavened bread started on the fifteenth day and lasted seven days, the first and last being a Sabbath. A regular Sabbath came in between. The day after that Sabbath began the feast of first fruits; it was always on the first day of the week. These feasts signified the coming Messiah and his kingdom (Colossians 2:16–17). Christ is our first fruits (1

Corinthians 15:23). On the first day of the week, we break bread and give thanks. It's a thanksgiving day.

The Sabbath in the Days of Christ

It says that the man that keeps the law shall live in them, but the just shall live by faith; the law is not of faith (Galatians 3:12). Only Jesus ever kept the law. The law condemns us all. The law is good, but it is bad news for sinners. In that way, it points to Christ, the end of the law. Moses spoke of a prophet to come like himself. *"It shall come to pass, that every soul, which will not hear that prophet, shall be destroyed from among the people"* (Acts 3:23). The law came by Moses, but grace and truth came by Jesus Messiah (John 1:17). If you fail to discern between the Old and New Testament, maybe you don't listen to him. Praise God, if you are Christ's you belong to Abraham, the household of faith, not to Moses (Galatians 3:29).

We give thanks for a promise fulfilled. On the mount of transfiguration, Peter, James, and John accompanied Jesus when a voice came from heaven, *"This is my beloved Son: hear him"* (Luke 9:35). God identified Jesus as the prophet of which Moses had spoken. Peter, writing about this event, says even so, *"We have also a more sure word of prophecy"* (2 Peter 1:19). We can trust the Scriptures.

Now, in Matthew 5 Jesus starts his ministry with the beatitudes. Only after them does he discuss the law. *"As his custom was, he went into the synagogue on the sabbath day"* (Luke 4:16) and fulfilled the law. Take note, though, that the word for "fulfill" means "to make full, to complete." Jesus did this by pointing out that mere observance is not sufficient. It has to come from a pure heart, from a love toward God, from repentance. All the more, we know that we have come short of the glory of God and need a Saviour. He said, "It has been told you, but I say unto you." That brings those commandments into perspective. How shall he improve on the fourth commandment; by picking another day, making another law? Really, *"if there had been a law given which could have given life, verily righteousness should have been by the law"* (Galatians 3:21).

He does not mention the fourth commandment here, but he promises rest for our souls in Matthew 11:28–29 and gives a new commandment in John 13:34 to love one another. It is the fulfilling of the law (Romans 13:10, Matthew 22:40).

All Scripture is God-breathed. All Scripture in the New Testament is not New Testament. A testament is only in force after the death of the testator. He has paid the price. *"This is my body, which is broken for you..."* (1 Corinthians 11:24). *"This is my blood... shed for you"* (Mark 14:24). *"This do in remembrance of me"* (Luke 22:19, 1 Corinthians 11:24). That is why Galatians 3:29 speaks of heirs. The Promised Land is an inheritance—we did not earn it. Call on Jesus, grab on to him, rather than a Sabbath. *"When he had by himself purged our sins, [he] sat down on the right hand of the Majesty on high"* (Hebrews 1:3). The job was done. God has spoken "in these last days," for all has been done. Our Lord and God said, "It is finished." And he rests till his enemies are made his footstool. The Sabbath is the last day of the week; we live in the last dispensation. Also in this respect, the spiritual comes last (1 Corinthians 15:46). Christ makes intercession until he will come down to judge the quick and the dead. After he comes for us, intercession ceases.

If a man be in Christ, he is a new creature; old things have passed away; all things are new (2 Corinthians 4:17). He is born again. How fitting it is that John starts his gospel with *"In the beginning was the Word, and the Word was with God, and the Word was God"* (John 1:1). The coming of Christ was that momentous. A new creature comes with a new creation. God indeed had done *"a new thing"* (Numbers 16:30, Isaiah 43:19, Jeremiah 31:22).

THE FIRST DAY OF THE WEEK IN THE NEW TESTAMENT

The New Testament testifies to the first day of the week. Jesus had risen on that day (Mark 16:9). The disciples had the doors locked for fear of the Jews. Suddenly Jesus was in the midst of them, and their mourning was changed into joy. *"Then were the disciples glad"* (John 20:20). They had seen no ghost. It was He.

A week later (eight days), they were together again (John 20:26). The doors were locked. Their fear did not come in intervals of seven days. This time Thomas was there, too, and Jesus showed himself again. He could have shown himself to Thomas as soon as Thomas opened his mouth. He waited not for the Sabbath, but for the first day of the week. Our Lord and God blessed and sanctified the day by his presence. Thomas agreed by saying, *"My Lord and my God"* (John 20:28). John 20:19–28 tells us about this. How good it is for brethren to dwell together in unity; there the Lord commands his blessing (Psalms 133). Forsake it not.

In Acts, the Holy Ghost descends on the first day of the week. The disciples were all together again. Again God blessed the day by his presence. On that day, the Church was born, not on the Sabbath before it. Isaiah 66:8 foretold it: *"Who hath heard such a thing? who hath seen such things? Shall the earth be made to bring forth in one day? or shall a nation be born at once? for as soon as Zion travailed, she brought forth her children."* It is a new day.

In Acts 20, Paul came to Troas and stayed seven days. On the first day of the week, not on the Sabbath, the disciples came to break bread. They worshipped on that day, remembering Jesus. Luke does not tell us they came to say goodbye to Paul. That's a myth. *"And upon the first day of the week, when the disciples came together to break bread..."* (Acts 20:7). It is not that they came together just that day, but on the first day of the week they used to get together all the time. Paul came there just a bit too late for the previous assembly, and had to wait.

In 1 Corinthians 16:1–2, Paul tells the believers to lay aside with them on the first day of the week as the Lord has prospered. He had given the same order in all the churches of Galatia; this is not just an offhand remark. The Scriptures are inspired of God.

We see then that John, Luke, and Paul testify to worship on the first day of the week. The Scriptures tell us that by the word of two or three witnesses a testimony shall stand (John 8:17).

In Acts 3 and 4, we get some idea of preaching. What was preached? Jesus! Four times we read that they preached the Word: the resurrection of Jesus. Should preaching then be central, or should the Eucharist be central? It could be a difference of religion and worship. Just don't leave out the blood. Can we skip the blood in the Eucharist?

Struggles

In John 16:12–14, Jesus tells his disciples that after the Holy Ghost came they would understand things that during his lifetime they could not bear. In Acts 15 we find that, even though they had been warned, they had difficulty bearing some of these things. Indeed, the Church still struggles to this day.

Now, the Sabbath, being part of the Ten Commandments, the law, is one of the things the Church struggles with. *"But there rose up certain of the sect of the Pharisees which believed, saying, that it was needful to circumcise them [the Gentiles], and to command them to keep the law of Moses"* (Acts 15:5). In the end, the Gentiles get instructions, but the fourth commandment is not even mentioned. On this occasion, Peter testifies, *"God, which knoweth the hearts, bare them witness, giving them the Holy Ghost, even as he did unto us; and put no difference between us and them, purifying their hearts by faith. Now therefore why tempt ye God, to put a yoke upon the neck of the disciples, which neither our fathers nor we were able to bear?"* That yoke he speaks of refers to the law of Moses, not just to circumcision. Circumcision is no hardship, no yoke.

In Galatians 4, Paul explains that the law was temporary, that until Christ came they were as children held in bondage under the elemental things of the world. The Judaizers tried to bring them again into bondage of those things. Does not Paul say in Galatians 5:3 that he who receives circumcision ought to keep the whole law? He is saying that the law is passed. Those who know the law are only driven to give up. They say, "If you have the name, play the game." (In other words, "You may as well live up to the name.") They know that the law is an unbearable yoke, as Peter called it, and Paul calls it *"the yoke of bondage"* (Galatians 5:1). Christ announced liberty to the captives. It is Good News to them that Christ has become our righteousness, our resting place. That's why publicans and whores go into the kingdom before the Pharisees. The Pharisees are bound to keep the law, but we are free!

In one church they would repeat the Ten Commandments every Sunday. They would not cook or go to a restaurant, get gas, or change a tire that day. They had replaced the Sabbath with a Sunday. When one minister had us repeat the beatitudes one day, he was "corrected" by his elders. Galatians 3:21 tells us that *"if there had been a law given which could have given life, verily righteousness should have been by the law."* We are under grace. The covenant of Sinai is obsolete (Hebrews 8:13). That's why I shrink back from a Sunday Sabbath. It's meant to be a rest, not a work. Where did God change the law? That's the wrong question. Why change?

If anyone wants to improve on God, that's blasphemous! That is tempting God. We have liberty in Christ and are free from the law of sin and death. Paul asks the Galatians, *"Having begun in the Spirit, are ye now made perfect by the flesh?"* (Galatians 3:3) Paul told the Galatians that their new gospel was no gospel at all. Accursed be he that would try to entangle you with a yoke of bondage again, that Christ should profit you nothing (Galatians 1:7–9, 5:1–4). In Galatians 5:22, no mention is made of the fourth commandment.

In Colossians, we read, *"Let no man therefore judge you... in respect of... the sabbath days"* (Colossians 2:16). That is any Sabbath, is it not? You think it does not refer to the Sabbath of the fourth commandment? Take note how almost all of the Ten Commandments are found in this book. You will not find the words "you shall" or "you shall not." No, we are under grace. In fact, the book is patterned after the Ten Commandments, the decalogue with its two tables. (Notice here that it refers to Jesus; he is God.) So the reference is to the fourth commandment and the Sabbaths of the law, not to heathen festivals (Colossians 2:14, 17). *"Let no man therefore judge you in meat, or in drink, or in respect of...the sabbath days,"* or call you a sun worshipper. Scripture is clear.

In Colossians 2:17, Paul goes on to say that these things are a shadow of things to come, but the body—the substance—is of Christ. Of course, heathen festivals never pointed to Christ. Shall we hold on to a shadow rather than the body? As we read in Colossians 2:10, in Christ (God) we are complete. We've been circumcised in him; we also rest in him.

We are born of Adam—but better yet, we are born again of the Word; in Christ, the last Adam, are our roots. We are seated with him in heavenly places. We have passed from death unto life. Today is the day of salvation. We shall rejoice and be glad in it. *"Christ in you, the hope of glory"* (Colossians 1:27). Don't glory in shadows or look through a veil or hold on to a promise as though it is still coming. That was fine under the Old Testament, but Christ our Sabbath—our promised rest, the light, the body, the gift—is here! If anyone thinks they can help Christ, he has failed to enter in and has come short of the promise (Acts 13:23, 32, and 26:6–7). *"Let us therefore fear, lest, a promise being left us of entering into his rest, any of you should seem to come short of it"* (Hebrews 4:1).

Did an angel tell you, "What are you doing polluting my holy day?" (Meaning the seventh day.) Remember, God does not contradict his Word, but Satan will show himself as an angel of light (2 Corinthians 11:14). He is a liar from the beginning, and the father of lies.

Conclusion

The Sabbath pointed to the deliverance of Israel out of Egypt (Deuteronomy 5:15). Jeremiah 23:7 tells us that in the days of the Branch—and those days are now—they will no more say, *"The Lord liveth, which brought up the children of Israel out of the land of Egypt."* Sabbatists, by keeping the Sabbath, still say that. That deliverance from Egypt was very great, but *"even that which had been made glorious had no glory in this respect, by reason of the glory that excelleth"* (2 Corinthians 3:10). The deliverance from Egypt was by the hand of God's servant Moses; ours is by the Son. See also Isaiah 43:18–19, Jeremiah 31:31–32.

The blood of Christ is precious. It cannot be compared with that of a man, a sinner. When God said, *"This is my beloved Son,"* those are God's words, not a man's. When God gave his Son, he did it all. To expect more would hold the blood in low esteem. By the same token, hell is forever, not just for a finite period of time. To differ with that would make it a question of how cheap is the blood. Without the shedding of blood, there is no remission of sin, and there is no salvation outside of Christ. He is the Saviour.

Christians should really devote the first day of the week to the Lord. That day points to the gift, the Saviour and Deliverer, the new creation, rather than to a promise of all that. It follows from the first commandment to love the Lord first of all. It and the breaking of bread in remembrance of Jesus are a clear testimony to Jesus, if we be Christians. He that has the Son has life, and he that has not the Son has not life. John, in Revelation, refers to this day as the Lord's Day. Yet there is no law mandating this. Give him the glory.

In his book *Sunday the First of the Sabbaths*, Charles Wesley Ewing shows that the early Christians kept the first days of the week as their day of worship. He quotes several authors from the book *The Ante—Nicene Fathers*, such as Ignatius, Barnabas, and Justin Martyr. He shows that Sunday was known as the day of the Lord, and that Constantine did not change the day of worship, but authorized the Sunday because it had been the day of worship from the beginning. Practice agreed with Scripture.[118]

"It is finished!" (John 19:30)

---

118 Ignatius (A.D. 30–107). Epistle to the Magnesians, Chapters VIII, IX, and X. Accessed: 9 November 2010 (http://www.searchgodsword.org/)

CHAPTER ELEVEN

THE ARAB-IRAELI CONFLICT

A LETTER TO SOME SABBATISTS

I have been thinking about writing to you for some time, but where to start? I'll start where we left off.

I referred to Acts 15:5, which one of you said I quoted out of context. I do not think so. Certain *Pharisees* from Jerusalem told the church they had to be circumcised and keep the law of Moses. The upshot was that they told them both in writing and face to face to observe certain things. Keeping the Sabbath is not mentioned among those, is it? The Ten Commandments are part of the law of Moses, are they not?

What does it mean that the New Testament mentions the Sabbath? Jesus went to the synagogue on the Sabbath, because he kept the law; no one else ever did. He was born under the law and kept it. Some apostles went to the synagogue. Did Jesus tell them not to? No, but he told them to preach the gospel to *"every creature"* (Mark 16:15). That includes the Jews, hallelujah. They meet in the synagogue on the Sabbath.

I do not mean to preach fornication, or other careless disregard for what others are used to observing (Acts 15:20). There is no room for lawlessness. Let repentance be honest, let it bring forth fruit. Grace is not cheap. All the law is fulfilled in this, you shall love your neighbour as yourself (Galatians 5:14). Remember also Romans 3:8, where Paul says: *"Why not rather, (as we be slanderously reported, and as some affirm that we say,) Let us do evil, that good may come?"* We have been called to liberty, not to use our freedom as an occasion to the flesh. Keeping the first day of the week is hardly such an occasion.

About Judaizers and the law, Paul says, *"Cast out the bondwoman and her son: for the son of the bondwoman shall not be heir with the son of the freewoman"* (Galatians 4:30). The present Jerusalem is *"in bondage with her children"* (Galatians 4:25). We have been warned to watch out for the leaven of the Pharisees (Matthew 16:6). We deal with that here. Read Galatians 5:1–16. Verse 9 tells us that a little leaven leavens the whole lump.

I have read your document, *How Did the Church Get So Far Removed from its Jewish Roots?* (You distributed that.) In 1 Corinthians 14:3, it says that prophecy is for edification, for exhortation and for comfort—that is, for encouragement. In the document there is no edification, and there is no comfort; is there exhortation? Should we not apply Galatians

5:15? *"But if ye bite and devour one another, take heed that ye be not consumed one of another."*

In the document, is Christ magnified at all? I don't see it. In my book, I wrote about the Sabbath and I glorified Christ. I will rejoice in the Lord (Philippians 3:1), and boast of him, not in the law. Does anything in the book not accord with Scripture? Does God contradict himself?

In Acts 15:24, we read about the Pharisees *"subverting your souls, saying Ye must...keep the law: to whom we gave no such commandment."* Will you now help them in this subversion? Will you now justify them?

The apostles had a charge to preach the Good News to every creature. We read that they preached Jesus (Colossians 1:28, Acts 2:22–36). That's why, when the Holy Ghost came down, they spoke in other tongues, not particularly in Latin or Hebrew. That happened on the first day of the week (Acts 2:1). God's glorious Church was born. On that day, we say thanks and remember Christ's commandment; we break bread, just like the early churches (1 Corinthians 16:1–2, Revelation 1:10, Acts 20:7). It is not law; we are under grace.

The document is highly critical of great men. If we want to criticize, we could criticize Paul, Daniel, David, Moses, Noah, and Adam; they all fell short. Paul boasted in Jesus, not in the law. Peter, talking about the law, said, *"Now therefore why tempt ye God, to put a yoke upon the neck of the disciples, which neither our fathers nor we were able to bear?"* (Acts 15:10).

You may protest, but by separating yourself from those who worship on Sunday I think that you condemn them. God put no difference between them, purifying their hearts by faith (Acts 15:9). Even stronger, *"What God hath cleansed, that call not thou common,"* three times over (Acts 10:15). So far.

A Response to a Book

It is a myth to teach that we have to keep the law of Moses. We saw it in the letter. In Galatians, Paul is saying that if we want to go by part of the law, we have to keep the whole. Mythmaking is not dead today, and we see it in *The Mountains of Israel* by Norma Parrish Archbold.[119] Parrish caters to the Jews and wants us to cater to them, but she is wrong about this.

You can tell a lot from the foreword of a book. Zola Levitt wrote one for this book. The foreword starts off with, "A profound ignorance exists concerning what is taking place in the land of Israel." I agree, but more serious, a profound ignorance exists of Scripture. Jesus said that where the dead body is, there the vultures gather (Matthew 24:28). Ignorance makes us vulnerable to lies.

Jesus came to destroy the works of the devil (1 John 3:8). He still does through his people. Ezekiel was told as much as "Son of man, stand up and pay attention" (Ezekiel 2:1). He had to eat a scroll. It was written on both sides (Ezekiel 2:8), meaning that one could not take away one part without taking away another. The Word cannot be broken. The

---
[119] Archbold, Norma Parrish. *The Mountains of Israel*. Foreword by Zola Levitt.

Church has an important responsibility and should speak out; judgment begins at the house of God (1 Peter 4:17). God made Ezekiel a watchman to Israel (Ezekiel 3:17). Everyone is responsible for himself; there is no such thing as "once saved, always saved," but if you do not warn the wicked, *"his blood will I require at thine hand"* (Ezekiel 3:18).

In Ezekiel, the false prophets said of the prophecy, *"It is not near; let us build houses"* (Ezekiel 11:3). Today they say, "The end is not near for at least a thousand years; let us build Israel."

Since we are dealing with a physical and spiritual Israel, we have to distinguish which is meant, or which we mean. Only spiritual Israel really counts today. Paul says that the natural comes first, then the spiritual (1 Corinthians 15:46). God will not go back to a natural kingdom. The kingdom of God does not come with observation (Luke 17:20). We find it in men's hearts; it is spiritual. Jesus said that his kingdom is not of this earth (John 18:36).

Paul says, in Romans 9:6–8, *"They are not all Israel, which are of Israel: neither, because they are the seed of Abraham, are they all children: but, in Isaac shall thy seed be called. That is, they which are the children of the flesh, these are not the children of God: but the children of the promise are counted for the seed."* Since the Jews are not the children of God, neither are they heirs. Paul, in Romans 11:15, asks, *"What shall the receiving of [the Jews] be, but life from the dead?"* Said in another way, don't expect conversion en masse; only a remnant will be saved. (See also Romans 11:4–5, 7, 14–15, or 28.)

Be careful not to walk after the flesh, but after the Spirit. They who walk according to the flesh cannot please God. To be carnally minded is enmity against God, but to be spiritually minded is life and peace. John the Baptist told the Pharisees, *"Think not to say within yourselves, We have Abraham to our father: for I say unto you, that God is able of these stones to raise up children unto Abraham"* (Matthew 3:9). John knew the Jews preferred to walk after the flesh. Who, Jew or Arab, walks after the Spirit? Peter stated that men are willingly ignorant (2 Peter 3:5). It's their choice. Without God, the builders build in vain (Psalms 127:1); without him, there will always be "peace negotiations." Christ is the chief cornerstone.

Paul reflected Jesus. Jesus talked with the Jews who claimed they were Abraham's seed (John 8:33). Jesus says, *"If ye were Abraham's children, ye would do the works of Abraham"* (John 8:39). He plainly tells them, *"Ye are of your father the devil"* (John 8:44). That goes for everyone not born of the Spirit.

Jesus said, *"Search the scriptures; for [they]… testify of me"* (John 5:39). Worthy is the lamb of all glory, *"for thou hast created all things, and for thy pleasure they are and were created"* (Revelation 4:11). In other words, Scripture speaks first of all about Jesus, hidden since the foundation of the world (Matthew 13:35), not about the Jews.

In *The Mountains of Israel*, the author never mentions that Abraham looked for a city whose founder and builder is God. Because they looked for such a city, therefore Abraham lived in Canaan as a stranger with Isaac and Jacob, dwelling in tents (Hebrews 11:9–10). Why did she not mention that? If we are to look for the Promised Land as a piece of real estate, we are presented with the most cunningly devised fable ever. Are we all to share in this real estate? Since they are not all Jews which are of Israel, is the Promised Land as real estate really for them and not rather for the Christians? I am just fine where I am. Anyway, Paul says that the promise to Abraham was that he would be heir of the world (Romans 4:13). Certainly, for Israel in the flesh the Promised Land is not their inheritance, which can be theirs only by faith.

Natural Israel does not fulfill the promise of Abraham. Isaiah 34—35 does not talk about natural Israel. The nations addressed in Isaiah 35 are all the nations, including spiritual Israel, of the world today. The world has only two kinds of people—the citizens of heaven (Ephesians 2:6, Hebrews 12:22) and the inhabitants of the world (Revelation 11:10).

Peter repeats the final destruction of the earth, of Isaiah 34:4, and he obviously refers to when Christ returns. Zion, in Isaiah 35:10, is spiritual Israel. 2 Peter 3:2 admonishes, *"That ye may be mindful of the words which were spoken before by the holy prophets, and of the commandment of us the apostles of the Lord and Saviour."* (See Ephesians 2:20, Jude 17.) That sounds to me as though we better interpret the Bible from the New Testament rather than from the Old Testament. In this book, how much is quoted from the New Testament? Very little. We should remember that in the beginning was the Word (Jesus) and that we were chosen in Christ from before the foundation of the world. Jesus is the chief cornerstone, the first and the last—he is not an afterthought (Acts 15:18, Titus 1:2, Revelation 13:8).

Our God is one. The Spirit and Christ are one. To be spiritually minded means to walk after Christ. Isaiah, besides calling Christ the mighty God and everlasting Father, calls him the Prince of peace (Isaiah 9:6–7). In him the lion and the lamb, Jew and Arab, will lie down together. They cannot lie down together in peace as long as one party carries a sword. They that live by the sword shall die by the sword (Matthew 26:52). A jihad with the sword means death. As long as the Jews cast their eyes on "what was promised to us," there cannot be peace. If they live by the sword, they will also die by it.

Of Israel, Paul says that only a remnant shall be saved (Romans 9:27). Paul quotes Isaiah, saying, *"Except the Lord of hosts had left unto us a very small remnant, we should have been as Sodom, and we should have been like unto Gomorrah"* (Isaiah 1:9). That would contradict his saying that all Israel will be saved, if we understand *"all Israel"* to refer to natural Israel (Romans 11:26). In Romans 11:28, Paul says that as touching the election (only some of natural Israel), they are beloved for the fathers' sakes. Praise the Lord for his grace.

Revelation 11:8 says, *"Their dead bodies shall lie in the street of the great city, which spiritually is called Sodom and Egypt, where also our Lord was crucified."* That is quite different from how many think of it, the Holy City. See also Revelation 2:9 and Revelation 3:9. John [Christ] speaks there of those who claim to be Jews, but are the synagogue of Satan.

Before the exile to Babylon there were two nations. There was definitely only one afterward. Ezekiel lived in Babylon. In Ezekiel 37, he prophesied a new Israel (spiritual) with a new heart, as Jeremiah did in Jeremiah 31:31. Ezekiel talks about the children for many generations; Peter also said on the day of Pentecost, *"For the promise is unto you, and to your children"* (Acts 2:39). David shall be their prince (king) forever (Ezekiel 37:24). Ezekiel 37:26–27 gives the same promises Jesus himself makes, and they reappear in many other parts of the New Testament. Ezekiel 37:28 refers to spiritual Israel, as is obvious from *"my sanctuary shall be in the midst of them for evermore."* It is Christ in you, the hope of glory. He dwells with his people, not in a manmade temple.

Jesus said, *"I am come that they might have life, and that they might have it more abundantly"* (John 10:10). That applies to his followers. To transfer these promises to physical Israel makes the Bible a myth.

Some will say that I spiritualize everything, or they will call this replacement theology (see below). They are proud to be literalists. Of course, they agree that, in Matthew 17, Christ compared Elijah to John the Baptist. John himself said that he was not Elijah. I am saying that Ezekiel 37 speaks of David, though we understand that it refers to Jesus. The Old Testament spoke in spiritual terms for good reasons. If the princes of this world had known it, they would not have killed Jesus (1 Corinthians 2:8). We have to understand God's code. Let those who have ears, *"Hear, and understand"* (Matthew 15:10).

Genesis 49:10 says that *"the sceptre shall not depart from Judah, nor a lawgiver from between his feet, until Shiloh come; and unto him shall the gathering of the people be."* This Shiloh, he that is worthy, is none other but Jesus. Spiritual Israel will gather to him. He was born king of the Jews and so he was crucified. Mary received the prophecy that the Lord God would give him the throne of his father David and of his kingdom there will be no end (Luke 1:32–33). Truly, it has happened. Shall we not praise him? These verses are skipped in *The Mountains of Israel* and we get less than *"truth in the inward parts"* (Psalms 51:6).

In many passages, also Isaiah 35, the Promised Land is pictured as a land flowing with milk and honey—in other words, it prospers. It is fulfilled in Christ. He said, *"I am come that they might have life, and that they might have it more abundantly"* (John 10:10). In Isaiah 35:8, the highway is none but Christ. *"I am the way"* (John 14:6). Only the ransomed of the Lord shall travel this highway. Nothing shall cause harm on God's holy mountain (in God's kingdom). Acts 15:15–18 interprets the prophets. The tent of David will be rebuilt. The Lord makes these things known from of old. I will accept that.

Looking at the present reality in Israel, what shall we say? The builders build in vain without Christ. This world is ready to disappear (2 Peter 3:14). There will not be any real estate. Nothing is new, only Christ is still Good News, to Jews and Gentiles. Give him the glory.

A Response to Another Book

The term "replacement theology" is a label which only its foes apply, not its friends. According to John Hagee, it is "the idea that the church has replaced the nation of Israel and the Jews in the economy of God."[120] He cites James Parkes, who says that the Christian Church with this idea is responsible for the deliberate murder of six million Jews and that replacement theology "has its ultimate resting place in the teaching of the New Testament itself."[121]

The term is quite understandable. After all, who is a Jew, but the one who belongs to Jesus? (Romans 2:28–29) Paul calls this entity the church of God. In Galatians, he uses the terms *"Jerusalem which is above"* (Galatians 4:26), *"the household of faith"* (Galatians 6:10), and *"the Israel of God"* (Galatians 6:16). In Ephesians 2:12, he talks about *"the commonwealth of Israel."* Indeed, it has happened: Abraham is heir of the whole world. Maybe we ought to talk about implant theology rather than replacement theology. Paul talks about grafting in Romans 12:17. Without implant theology, the Old Testament would largely have no meaning for Christians.

Hagee, in "Defense of Israel," a book meant for Christians, caters to the Jews and even has a rabbi give the foreword. I wonder if in Jesus' place, tempted by the devil, he would not have said, "All right, give me the kingdoms." He may not

---
120 Hagee, John. In defense of Israel, (Lake Mary, Florida, FrontLine, A Strang company, 2007), p.121.
121 Ibid, p.125.

mean that, but he sounds like it. Maybe Hagee forgot not to walk in the counsel of the ungodly. He who does not have the Son, though he be a rabbi, neither has the Father.

He claims Jesus refused to be their Messiah. Peter acknowledged him as such, and the Lord said, *"Blessed art thou"* (Matthew 16:17). Martha also said the same (John 11:27). Jesus agreed. Daniel prophesied Jesus' kingdom (Daniel 2:44). If he refused, he refused it on their terms. Peter had to be corrected; he preferred the things of men above the things of God (Matthew 16:23). I am afraid Hagee is in the same boat as Peter was. Jesus was and is both Messiah and Saviour of the whole world, including the Jews.

He reigns over the house of Jacob, and of the increase of his government there shall be no end. Peter told the Jews that they had crucified and slain by wicked hands him who was approved of God by miracles in their midst (Acts 2:18). They were guilty (compare this to Leviticus 5:1–2). In verse Acts 2:36, Peter told them that they had crucified their Lord and Messiah. They agreed and repented.

At the beginning of his ministry, Jesus said, *"Repent: for the kingdom of heaven is at hand"* (Matthew 4:17). Jesus was the king, and John the Baptist had heralded his coming. It was at the time of the fourth kingdom, the kingdom of iron of the image in the book of Daniel. The kingdom was large and difficult to keep together; it was mixed iron and clay. The kingdom of heaven came with peace, without hands. Jesus was its King, and of the increase of his kingdom is no end; this kingdom fills the whole earth. It shall stand forever. The gates of hell shall not prevail against it. It will not be left to other men. Jesus said, *"I will build my church."* (Matthew 16:18). The stone broke the iron, the brass, the clay, the silver, and the gold into pieces which the wind carried away (Daniel 2:45). They represent the kingdoms of the earth which have a time and a season; they come to an end. Do the elements vanish in the reverse order of their coming because Jesus is the foundation of the kingdom of heaven, and not an afterthought?

The natural comes first, then the spiritual. Daniel told the king, *"There is a God in heaven that revealeth secrets, and maketh known to the king Nebuchadnezzar what shall be in the latter days"* (Daniel 2:28). On the day of Pentecost, Peter told the crowd, quoting the prophet Joel, *"And it shall come to pass in the last days"* (Acts 2:17). In Hebrews 1:2, it says that God has spoken to us *"in these last days."* The spiritual kingdom has come; it is here. We live in the last days.

Epilogue

In the beginning, God created all things out of nothing. He made the earth to be inhabited. He made man like himself, and it was very good (Genesis 1). God rested from all his works and declared the seventh day holy (Genesis 2). Because Adam was like God, God could enjoy fellowship with him—*"the son of God,"* Luke says (Luke 3:38). God loved fellowship and delighted in his work and in his children, as we do in ours. Adam and Eve broke the fellowship.

In Christ, God restores fellowship. God is love, and God so loved the world that he gave his only Son, that whoever puts his trust in him should not perish but have life. The Son obeyed his Father perfectly (John 3:31–36). While we were yet sinners, Christ died for the ungodly, the damnable (Romans 5:6–8). The living God is jealous for his bride and wants a living and fruitful relationship with her (Genesis 1:28). He himself, Christ, is the first sacrifice and the first fruit. Without the shedding of blood there is no remission of sin (Hebrews 9:22). The law came by Moses, but grace and truth came by Jesus Christ (John 1:17).

With Christ came a new creation, and all things were made new. In the beginning was the Word, and the Word was

God. Compare Genesis 1:1 and John 1:1. That Word needs to transform us. Unless we die to ourselves and rise with Christ (John 5:24), unless we be made alive to God through him (Colossians 2:12–13), there is no hope. Without faith in him, it is impossible to please God (Hebrews 11:6); there cannot be fellowship. This restored fellowship is obtained through inheritance, a testament. It cannot be obtained by works, by us earning it.

God can take a crooked stick and strike a straight blow. The Masoretic and Septuagint may not be entirely as originally given, but God uses them nonetheless. By the same token, God can make an ugly caterpillar and make from it a beautiful butterfly. He can change a persecutor of the Church into a Paul; make a wavering reed (Simon) into a rock (Peter). He is able to save to the uttermost.

Christ did not come to condemn the world, but to save it (John 3:17). God's promise to Abraham was first of all, *"I will bless them that bless thee"* (Genesis 12:3). He would rather do that than curse. God is not willing that any should perish, but that they should have life eternal.

We had to really dig for many of the facts we uncovered. Christ could have provided the names of the pharaohs, the true chronology, but he did not. When the ark is lost to the Philistines, Saul is not mentioned. Was it a matter of being wise as serpents and harmless as doves? Maybe it was a matter of not judging before the time. After all, Samuel anointed Saul and God chose Saul to *"save my people out of the hand of the Philistines"* (1 Samuel 9:16). God's thoughts are far higher than ours, but his thoughts toward us are good. God is love. He does not want to be a museum piece, to be known only from a book. Instead he wants for us to call on him and have a living relationship with him. He is ever ready to forgive. Even on the cross, Christ cried out, *"Father, forgive them; for they know not what they do"* (Luke 23:34). Prophecies, tongues, and knowledge shall vanish away, but faith, hope, and love abide, and the greatest of those is love (1 Corinthians 13:8–13).

"Come unto me, all ye that labour and are heavy laden, and I will give you rest." (Matthew 11:28)

Reindert de Jonge in bible by Uitg. Boekencentrum

CPSIA information can be obtained at www.ICGtesting.com
Printed in the USA
238112LV00004B/1/P